# Pursuit *of* Excellence

*14 Steps to Peak Performance*

ARUN SINGH

An imprint of
Srishti Publishers & Distributors

**Srishti Publishers & Distributors**
A unit of AJR Publishing LLP
212A, Peacock Lane
Shahpur Jat, New Delhi – 110 049

editorial@srishtipublishers.com

First published in India by Bold,
an imprint of Srishti Publishers & Distributors in 2023



10 9 8 7 6 5 4 3 2 1



Printed and bound in India

***Dedicated to***

***Babuji and Ma…***

*Who could not live to see the fruit of their struggle*

*But must be happy to see some more shine*
*spreading in the world.*

♠

# WHY I WROTE THIS BOOK

I decided to write this book after Arup Bose from Prabhat Publishers approached me to check if I would be interested in writing a book on self-improvement for students and first-time jobbers. I instantly said yes.

Hence, the credit behind writing this book – which I am sure, would be transforming the lives of many by inspiring them to take conscious actions – goes actually to him.

While going through the book, keep a diary with you and jot down the key points from each of the chapters. Use a four-colour pen and use different colours while making notes. Make some drawings and sketches to make the notes more actionable. As you know, we see pictures before words and hence some sketches add greater value. That way, you will have your own summary note, based on which you can take actions at a faster pace.

And you will be a transformed, inspired and improved version of you very soon.

No doubt about it!

I have been working with many people, including [illegible] professionals, businessmen, sportspersons, musicians and students and can vouch for the magic which will unfold if you just sincerely try.

After reading this book, you should stay connected with me through any of my social media handles, including YouTube [illegible] 'Stay Inspired with Arun' and 'Transformed [illegible] by Arun' Facebook Page 'The Transformed You' and Instagram account [illegible]. You can also check my website [illegible] and [illegible].

# Contents

Acknowledgement .. .. .. .. .. .. .. .. .. .. .. .. .. .. .. .. .. .. .. .. .. .. . vii
Foreword .. .. .. .. .. .. .. .. .. .. .. .. .. .. .. .. .. .. .. .. .. .. .. .. .. xi
What this book is all about? .. .. .. .. .. .. .. .. .. .. .. .. .. .. ..xii
Why this book? . .. .. .. .. .. .. .. .. .. .. .. .. .. .. .. .. .. .. .. xvii
A note from the author .. .. .. .. .. .. .. .. .. .. .. .. .. .. .. .. .xxi

Chapter 1
The Questions I Hear the Most .. .. .. .. .. .. .. .. .. .. .. .. .. .. 1

Chapter 2
Hunger – Do you have it?. .. .. .. .. .. .. .. .. .. .. .. .. .. .. .. .. 5

Chapter 3
4 Types of Mindset .. .. .. .. .. .. .. .. .. .. .. .. .. .. .. .. .. .. .. 8

Chapter 4
Who am I? - A question worth answering .. .. .. .. .. .. .. .. ..19

Chapter 5
Coach and Company. .. .. .. .. .. .. .. .. .. .. .. .. .. .. .. .. .. .32

Chapter 6
Habits.. .. .. .. .. .. .. .. .. .. .. .. .. .. .. .. .. .. .. .. .. .. .. .. .38

Chapter 7
Discipline of taking actions (DOA).. .. .. .. .. .. .. .. .. .. .. .. ..77

Chapter 8
Health.. .. .. .. .. .. .. .. .. .. .. .. .. .. .. .. .. .. .. .. .. .. .. .. .98

Chapter 9
Common Issues which bother millennials .. .. .. .. .. .. .. .. .. 102

Chapter 10
One solution to all problems – MMRG .. .. .. .. .. .. .. .. .. .. .. .. .119

Chapter 11
10 Pitfalls you should guard against.. .. .. .. .. .. .. .. .. .. .. .. 126

Chapter 12
16 Commandments for Peak Performance .. .. .. .. .. .. .. .. .. .. 130

Chapter 13
How to stay motivated to be on the move? .. .. .. .. .. .. .. .. .. .. 135

Chapter 14
What is Human Transformation? – A recap.. .. .. .. .. .. .. .. .. 139

# Acknowledgement

I would like to extend my sincere gratitude to those from this universe who inspired me to write this book.

My heartfelt gratitude for the blessings of Swami Ramdev Ji Maharaj for all the seven books. His kind blessings and abundance of love for my purpose of transforming the lives of people gave me indomitable courage to keep moving.

My gratitude to Dr Nagendra Neeraj, Chief Medical In-charge of Yog Gram for his constant inspiration and support to let my inspiring thoughts reach out to numerous people. Whenever we met, we used to go for long forest and nature trails. During these walks, we used to talk about life, health, wellness, mindset, laws of the universe and the way people should live their life to feel the abundance within them.

I am indebted to Dr Manju Neeraj, Pragya, Soumya, and Medha for words of inspiration for all my writings. They have been my sounding boards for all my writings. I am grateful for their continued wishes and inspiration.

Thanks to Bishwamitra Singh, Urmila Singh, Sushil, Rajeev and Neelima for words of motivation which went a long way in presenting the second book in such a quick succession.

Special credits to A.M. Misra, Former Chairman Tata Sponge, TSKZN, India Steel & Wire Products, and Former Vice President

HR Tata Steel, who has been a life-long mentor and guide for me. As I said in my first book, I learnt from him that true and inspiring leaders exist in real life as well.

I would also like to mention a number of other people who played an instrumental role in my literary journey.

P.V. Rao, Chairman and MD, VP Synergic Weld Solutions and Ex Director, Pennar Industries Limited for his good wishes.

Hakimuddin Ali, Executive Director Cements, Dalmia Cement (Bharat) Ltd. for his constant motivation.

Rajiv Upadhyay, Managing Director, CHRYSO India for the words of motivation and good wishes.

U Ramachandran, ex General Manager of Tata Steel Limited, who kept sending his kind words to write and publish books.

Babuji, Ma and Jitendra bhaiya! Stay in peace wherever you are. I will fight with all my might to spread the shine of joys and success in the world around. Your goodness and blessings have made this possible.

My lovely wife Divya for taking charge of the home front in the days of working from home. That gave me some time to complete the books by utilising my time, which I otherwise used to spend while driving to and back from office. Thank you for the months of hard work which you also put in along with me, in our respective areas.

Thanks to the entire team from Srishti Publishers, with a special mention of Arup Bose and Stuti Gupta for an enriching association, which appears to be set for many decades to come.

Bhupenddra Singh Raathore sir for his constant mentoring and guidance. His teachings have been priceless and full of awakenings.

Dr Suresh Chandra Padhy, President (Vice Chancellor), Poornima University, Jaipur for ongoing association and opportunities to add more shine to the life of students and corporate leaders.

All my community members who join me at 5:30 a.m., three days every week in the ongoing '10x Success and Joys through the power of MMRG (Magical Morning Rituals for Greatness programme). It's an amazingly powerful and ever-growing group of people with a strong purpose to make their life and the life of people around them better.

And lastly, to anyone else who contributed to this book, whose name I might have missed mentioning. You are as important as the foundation pillars of a building. These are not visible, but the building cannot stand without these.

Together, let's make this world happier, healthier and better.

With love,
Arun Singh

# Foreword

Good leaders know themselves well and have a good clarity about what works best for them in life and career. As they move further on the path, they discover themselves better and realise more of their true potential. It all comes from a deep self-awareness and conviction for what is really important for someone.

There is no one formula of leadership and people discover the path better if they stay true to their own personalities and strengths. It is anyway going to be a journey of exploration, reflection and lots of unending hard work on the way.

Yes, having a good mentor or coach in life and career can be a deciding factor for one's success. Often, we see opportunities knocking at our door, but miss to 'see these as opportunities.' That is where a mentor adds value. However, it is often a challenge to get the right mentor.

Hence, it feels good to see a book on the fundamentals of self-awareness, self-coaching and self-leadership, as these are at the core of leading others later in life and profession.

To some extent, I will call this book, a book on self-mentoring.

While there are so many books on leadership already, there are just a few on how to turn to some of the basic age-old qualities of knowing our priorities well, focussing on just a few things at a time while working hard, and constantly working on our energy and the strength of character by learning and renewing ourselves.

This is because while everyone wants to lead, hardly anyone works on leading oneself.

Self-leadership forms the cornerstone of being a good leader. Mind you, it's a tough journey, as this also means that you are following your own heart and it may need some courageous and hard decisions on a regular basis.

Hope, books and ideas like this make the journey for the leaders of today and future a little easier. I am told, this book is primarily meant for young employees graduating afresh from MBA/other colleges who join corporates and try to figure out their own mantras of success. Mostly, they look around, copy others and try to do what most of the people around them seem to be doing.

My message to them would be – look within and build on your own experiences. And while exploring the world, do follow the fundamental principles of success, which are just a few.

I wish the book success and hope it will be of use to the readers. Though there are many books already available in the domain, let's take into consideration that the world is changing fast with breakthrough innovations and ideas. A part of us, which forms our belief and value system, remains the same, and another part evolves as we learn continuously. Hope this book helps the readers in both areas – to know who they are at the core; and to build on their abilities to learn, evolve and transform into better human beings.

*Amit Agrawal*
*Managing Director and CFO*
*Martrade Group, Middle East and India*

# What this book is all about?

I conduct sessions for groups of people, including employees from corporates and students from MBA colleges.

I always get inspired while thinking of the opportunity that we have in our hands by inspiring people in their early twenties to be good leaders later in their life.

They will become CEOs and CXOs and will bring a better work culture in corporates.

They will become the businessmen/businesswomen of tomorrow and will build a powerful work culture of empowerment, teamwork and contribution.

They will become the teachers who impart real value-based education to children, who in turn will shape a better India.

They will become parents and inculcate good values in their kids. They will teach their children how they can seek inspiration from things around them. How people can actually stay inspired by getting the lessons of inspiration from nature, people, experiences, books, videos and almost anything and everything. We will have future generations which can live in the moment and get a deeper meaning in food which they eat, conversations which they see and live, places they visit, books they read and projects they undertake. We will have more people who appreciate the goodness around them.

Hence, this book which is the first book of motivation, leadership and life improvement, specifically meant for students and first jobbers.

While conducting sessions for students, I have often come across one of the following questions:

- How to be confident on the stage?
- How to be a good public speaker?
- How to stay focussed in a world of reels and other content on social media?
- How to get one's dream job?
- How to move on from a break up?
- How to score high marks in examinations?
- How to build good relationships with family and friends?

The questions are many, but the solutions are just a few. One has to work on a few topics, and by doing so, one can become a transformed and stronger version of oneself.

This book has fourteen chapters and the readers should go through each of these at a leisurely pace. Go through one chapter at a time and think about the key lessons. Plan for taking actions on at least some of these and ideally on all the lessons. Share the summary of learnings with at least two people in your circle. This will help you strengthen the roots of learnings in your sub-conscious mind and the chances of you taking action will go up.

It's a book on the basic qualities of leading oneself and others, by working on which, young employees and senior students can build some of the foundations of being good and inspiring leaders.

In this book, the goal is to begin from basic needs which people are mostly thinking about (communication, positivity, energy, etc) and elevate their thinking to the higher levels of complete transformation (vision, habits, etc). Also, the idea is to give them some action blueprints by working on which they can get better in real life and work.

# Why this book?

I have written quite a few books. The book in your hands is the seventh one, to be precise. I have also co-authored books for others – mostly for CXOs and coaches – and if I include those, the number goes beyond a dozen.

I have created more than seven hundred videos and conducted many one-to-one coaching sessions.

Though each video is unique and each book has a specific message for the viewers, there is one common factor which binds all my creations together. It is the thread of 'inspiration'.

To make it specific, the central word is – 'Human Transformation for 10x Success and Joys'.

I also noticed that though there are many books written by motivational authors and many videos created by motivational speakers, there is hardly any book written for the life transformation of the younger generation. I mean, there is no book ever written specific to the needs of people in their early twenties. They may be students in engineering/MBA/other colleges or first-time jobbers who have recently joined a company and are looking for a book specific to their needs.

Hence, even after writing close to a dozen books, I decided to write on this particular theme.

I decided to write this book after Arup Bose from Srishti Publishers approached me to check if I would be interested in writing a book on self-improvement for students and first-time jobbers. I instantly said yes.

Hence, the credit behind writing this book – which I am sure, would be transforming the lives of many by inspiring them to take consistent actions – goes actually to him.

While going through the book, keep a diary with you and note down the key points from each of the chapters. Use a four-colour pen and use different colours while making notes. Make some creatives and sketches to make the notes more actionable. As you know, we see pictures before words and hence some sketches add greater value. That way, you will have your own summary note, based on which you can take actions at a faster pace.

And you will be a transformed, inspired and improved version of you very soon.

No doubt about it!

I have been working with many people, including corporate professionals, businessmen, sportspersons, musicians and students and can vouch for the magic which will unfold if you just give it a sincere try.

After reading this book, you should stay connected with me through any of my social media handles, including YouTube channels 'Stay Inspired with Arun' and 'Transformed You by Arun', Facebook Page 'The Transformed You' and Instagram account 'arunsingh1612'. You can also check my website www.authorcoacharun.com and www.coachauthorarun.com.

If you give this ample thought, you will realise that the company of people that you keep matters and you need to stay connected to gain maximum results. Even after you finish reading this book, the world of distraction will get you swayed away from your path. You will have to consciously stay at it.

I wish you enormous success in all aspects of your life. May the success you achieve as a result of reading this book and following the instructions inspire millions.

And do share the knowledge with others like you – students and first jobbers. You will become the channel to spread goodness around.

Stay great. Stay blessed.

# A note from the author

I am a serial author of motivational thrillers, life transformation coach and an on-the-spot motivational speaker. You might have noted that I have added a few prefixes before 'author', 'coach' and 'speaker'. I have done this after careful thinking and a progressive realization of a higher cause in front of me.

I wrote my first book in the year 2020. This book had some powerful action-based ideas which, if implemented in anyone's life, could have transformed someone's life permanently for the best. Even when the book was in the initial stages of copy editing, without waiting for a single day, I began writing my second book. As the second book went for copy editing, I began writing my third book and the world started changing in front of me in a magical way. I realized that the universe had granted me some powers which I had never earlier realized I possessed. It surely did not happen overnight; there was a journey of a few months of self-reflection, realization and taking consistent actions. And when I trace the path backwards, the *ever flowing motivation ki Ganga* as I always call my efforts, trickled out of the Gangotri of 'my Pietermaritzburg moment. It was about a painful and unpleasant experience which gave me the first nudge to come out of my comfort zone of decades and which keeps feeding fuel to the fire of inspiring the world and making people transform their life.

When I am writing these words today in 2023, I am filled with a deep sense of gratitude towards the universe which has given me – after three years of consistent actions and learnings – my first viral video which is being seen by 10,000 new people every hour even as I am writing these words. It has been seen by more than 1 lakh people in the last sixteen hours and is going to be seen by more than millions of people in the next few days. I always told my family and community members that very soon my videos are going to be seen by crores of people and today marks a new inning in my journey to help people transform their lives. I had recorded my first video three years ago in the year 2019. Today, after recording more than 600 videos, after learning many lessons on the way, and after constantly taking corrective actions, I see the first viral videos. As the *Bhagvat Gita* says – do your karma and take consistent actions; leave the responsibility of giving desired results, i.e. fruits in the hands of god. Taking consistent actions, while learning on the way, is in your hands. Giving the fruit of your labour is in the hands of god.

Dreams do come true. God, universe or the higher power does magic in your life after watching you for some good time...

Before the magic happens, you need to develop insights, realisations and understanding of how the world functions and then you need to take some actions. You often have to take massive actions and keep moving forward. You need to have patience.

There is no shortcut to success, many people might have told you. It however, does not help you much as people do not tell you the exact recipe for success and attainment of your dreams.

But you need not worry now. You have a book in your hands which will reveal to you all that you need to care for and do something about.

Success, greatness, health and joys will be yours.

Congratulations for this one decision of yours which will be the best decision you would ever have taken.

This one decision of buying this book is going to unlock the door to mega success and joys.

I am saying now and I think people will realize it in some time – it's just a matter of time – you have in your hands, one of the most inspiring and powerful books which you can ever get on this topic. I am saying this with humility. I am saying this with deep conviction. Read the book, reflect on the learnings and take action. You might have read or heard about some of the following quotes and sentences.

*Fortune favours the brave.*

*God helps those who help themselves.*

*You get luckier as you take more actions.*

I am there with you, holding your hand and walking along with you.

But are you ready to walk along?

Take actions and see the magic unfold in your life.

# Chapter 1

## The Questions I Hear the Most

I have worked in the corporate world for many years. For twenty-five years to be precise. I have had the opportunity of working in some of the most prestigious corporate houses in my tenure before I got into the field of serial-writing of motivational thrillers, life transformation coaching and, on-the-spot motivational speaking. Coincidentally, when I came to this field, my first series of talks happened in a university where, for the first time in my life and career, I designed and delivered a day-long motivational programme for senior level MBA students. It was the first time I tested my passion and commitment for bringing awareness and inspiration in the lives of students. My programmes were also attended by some senior faculty members. I knew this is where I belonged . God had unleashed the hidden powers, hitherto unknown even to me, to help people working in corporates and studying in colleges discover their true powers and build a life and career which would have been many times bigger and more fulfilling than the life they would have chosen for them.

I also realized a very remarkable secret, which so far I had not paid attention to. I found that most of the people discover their true purpose and passions for life after they have led half their life. This happened with me as well. I discovered my true powers when I was forty-four years of age. I was not doing well for me and my family till then. I was in fact doing great, but I was oblivious of the fact that there was another field where I could have achieved much more. I realized this after attending a two-day programme called 'Discover Your Vision'. When I attended this programme, I realized – I should have attended this at least a decade or two ago. Then I also realized the power of seven secrets of success and happiness which became the basis of my first book.

Once I started discovering my true inner powers, I became a serial author and on-the-spot motivational speaker, who could have inspired people at any place without any slide or pre-work. The whole world became a place for me to seek and share inspiration. People started to connect with me. I began coaching them and giving motivational talks.

Then I had an idea – why don't we teach all these secrets of self-transformation and empowerment to students from colleges and first-time jobbers. If these people, who are in their early or late twenties, are exposed to the secrets of self-awareness, self-discovery and secrets of success and happiness, they will have the freedom to choose the field where they truly belong.

The more I reflected on this awareness, the more I got excited and inspired to write a book especially dedicated to the young college students and first-time jobbers. I had also decided to conduct a series of sessions for students from various MBA and other colleges in various states of the country. While touring different places and speaking with the students, I realized how relevant this initiative was

– of bringing transformation into the lives of youngsters when they needed it the most.

I used to come across a few recurrent questions from numerous students while conversing with students and young people who were new to corporate careers. I also keep receiving many questions because I conduct my programmes in an interactive manner, while engaging the young audience in a series of conversations. I ask questions, guide them to think on their feet, provoke them to think about the solutions and answers before I suggest the answers and inspire them while resolving some of their life's worries.

So, I have enlisted the frequently asked questions :

- How to speak English confidently?
- How to speak to strangers confidently?
- How to be better at public speaking?
- How to win over the fear of speaking?
- How to come out of a breakup?
- How to stay focussed and fall prey to distractions?
- How to choose the right professions?

Very few asked me how to be as successful as N.R. Narayana Murthy or Ratan Tata? Or how to be as disciplined as Virat Kohli. They all wanted to be as rich as Virat or Dhoni, but somehow very few actually came and discussed with me the steps to do something transformational and big in life.

I found a few students who wanted to become entrepreneurs. Just a few of them. But I also knew that as I visited more campuses, I would find more students who wanted to create something new and were ready to put in the kind of hard work which was required for them to follow their passion, discover their purpose, and set a legacy for others to follow.

Please do not get me wrong. I am not looking down upon others who have more common goals in life. When a person like me, who has excellent qualification (going by the definition put forth by the society) and is braced with the experience of working in some of the best known multinationals, discovered my true calling at the age of forty-four, who am I to look down upon others!

But I had understood one thing. As Maslow proposed his theory of hierarchy of needs, the students also had their own hierarchy. They absolutely reasonably, wanted first to find solutions to some of their immediate personal problems and then later on they would have been taking actions to transform their life to be their 2.0, 3.0 or N.0 version, and would have aspired to work at their peak potential. In other words, they would later on have worked on their self-transformation while discovering their vision and purpose of life, build some winning habits, set goals and had gone on taking actions to attain their massive goals. As in Maslow's hierarchy, first people look for the fulfilment of the physical needs before going for the pursuit of self-actualization. Here again, students and first-time jobbers initially wanted to settle in their life before thinking of doing something massive.

Hence, I have planned and written this book in such a manner that first we go through all the secrets of success for doing something really big in life. Then we will apply these concepts on the questions asked by the students. I am sure the readers will eventually get the answer to all their questions. They will also find all the secrets of life transformation.

# Chapter 2

## Hunger – Do you have it?

I've been coaching, lecturing, and writing to motivate individuals to improve their lives and can attest to one trait that makes all the difference. Surprisingly, this quality emerges from within you rather than from the outside environment. You certainly possess this quality or else you would never have picked this book for reading.

I call this quality 'hunger'.

An insatiable hunger for growth and greatness.

Let's begin the journey of understanding this quality with an example.

I live in the beautiful city of Pune. Imagine that you have just come to visit my home after a long time and I am keen to treat you nicely. I want to make you feel special and in my over-enthusiasm, I prepare and order some nice delicacies. I arrange on the dining table all fifty-six delicacies, better known as *chhappan bhog* in India. In case you think it's too unrealistic for an example, okay! Suppose I bring down the number of delicacies to five. Whatever be the spread of some mouth-watering cuisine on the table or whatever be the quality of preparation, will you eat and relish the food if you have already had a meal?

Here comes 'hunger' in the framework of discussion now.

If you are hungry, you will enjoy eating even if I offer you five food items.

However, if your stomach is full and you are not hungry, you will not enjoy even if I offer you a chhappan bhog to eat.

It's the same thing with this book.

The book has all the secrets of success which can be compared with chhappan bhog in the example given above.

But do you have the hunger to grow and succeed?

Do you have the hunger to make it big in life?

Do you have the hunger to first transform your life and then the lives of people around you?

Do you have the hunger to think, do, have and be more?

If yes, this book is for you.

And the very fact that you have a copy of this book in your hands shows that you surely have hunger within you.

I know, you want to grow in life.

I know, you want to succeed in life, business, career and the field of your choice.

I know, you want to have better health and more wealth.

I know, you want to make change in the way your life is happening around you.

I know, you are going to attain all of these and more.

Just be with me, read the book, reflect on the learnings and take actions. In case of queries, please feel free to reach out to me through one of my social media handles. As mentioned earlier in the book, you can connect with me through my website: www.authorcoacharun.com.

Welcome onboard.

Welcome to the world of joys, health and success through transformation of life...

...for the best of reasons!

And before you proceed, ask yourself the question – "Do I have the *hunger* to become great?"

# Chapter 3

## 4 Types of Mindset

You might have seen a common pattern among all successful people. You look at the best sportsmen, corporate leaders, spiritual gurus, writers, speakers, actors, journalists or political leaders who have reached the pinnacles of success. They always appear calmer and happier than others, all the time. Have you seen Mr N.R. Narayana Murthy, Azim Premji or Prime Minister Modi ever rattled by the volley of irritating questions in any forum? Have you seen Sadguru or Swami Ramdev getting angry with journalists? Have you seen Sachin Tendulkar and Dhoni ever losing their calm? Instead, they will always think on their feet and live in the moment. In fact, they have become great because when things get tougher, they show their true talents and potential. They are known for how they carry themselves when things become very challenging. Dhoni is known for match winning sixes often on the last ball of the last over. Virat Kohli is known for bouncing back every time people think he had reached the end of his career. He recently hit the first ODI century after a gap of around three years. This is too long a time for someone to have stayed out of form. This is just an example; the point here is

– world's best have a winning mindset. They shine more when/after things get tougher.

This brings us to the topic of having or developing a winning mindset.

## Winning Mindset

"Adversity is the mother of transformation", was the tagline on the cover page of my first motivational thriller – *My Pietermaritzburg Moment*. After completing my study of numerous success tales, I discovered that those who achieve are those who turn their most difficult experiences into the brightest success stories. When things are good, people attain just an average result. When things become so tough that the comfort zone of people is broken, people with a winning mindset get up and put in their best.

This way of thinking is what I call the winning mindset.

This is one of the four different forms of mindsets which anyone willing to do anything worthwhile and be happy and successful has to understand.

A person with a winning mindset will develop or have a 'different' way of looking at things. "Your perspective matters," you must have heard of this saying from a few people.

A rejection can mean the end of opportunities for you. But for people with a winning mindset, this could mean the beginning of new explorations. It is only because of the rejections that you are now exploring new avenues where unknown to you, bigger success is hiding. Rejection makes it uncomfortable for you, which in other words is similar to 'breaking of the comfort zone'. It's only then that you act differently.

Bad health can make you sad and suffer through illness. It can also mark the beginning of a healthier life if you make a change in your eating and living habits.

Lower than expected marks in an examination can mean disappointment and discouragement. It can also lead you to a decision of working harder so that you do much better in the upcoming examinations.

A breakup from the girl you loved can mean disappointment. It can also mean the beginning of new relationships as now you can spend some quality time with your parents, teachers, mentors, friends and other new relatives towards whom you got blinded after falling in love.

Bad news would make you sad; and you keep hearing lots of bad news from TV and newspapers. But these are also awakening you to the reality of a world which has a mix of good and bad and you need to be cautious. *Josh mein hosh mat khona* is what our ancestors said. They had a reason. If you get so excited that you lose sight of upcoming rejections, uncertainties and potholes, you are in for an accident. Hence bad news tells you – welcome to the real world where for every great guy you meet, there is a rogue lurking. You need to be careful. Both can be used to get better in life.

You lose your job in the ongoing recessions. It can mean a heartbreak. It can also mean the opening of a new world of opportunities. Now you can enrol yourself in a new course and add to your skills. You can also apply for bigger companies and, if asked, can tell them that it's related to the recession and does not have to do with your abilities. If you apply for one hundred companies, you will surely get through one of these. Or else, if you still do not get a job, may be make your Vision Board and discover yourself (I conduct a Vision Board exercise regularly for interested people. Just type 'Vision Board' and send a message to me. My team will connect with you.). This may transform your whole life, as you will understand yourself in a better way – in a way you never knew yourself. You will know your true self and abilities. You will know your hidden powers and will be more focussed to take actions to build the castle of your dreams on the foundation of your talents and passion. This experience of a sudden loss of job will also make you realize the frivolities of life and you will henceforth become a more planned person in terms of investment, career, health, etc. Perspective makes all the difference.

You were asked to give a speech on the stage and you could not deliver it. You got nervous. You could not connect with the audience. You felt bad. So what? You need to practice more often. You need to practise speaking by choosing a topic everyday and giving a speech in front of the selfie camera or a mirror. You need to make it a habit to speak for at least a minute every day. You ought to do some meditation in early morning hours, as it makes you smarter by giving you clarity of thought. It also teaches you to be in the moment and stay calm. It makes you a better speaker by helping with more neural connections in your mind.

You do not have a rich family background. You see some of your friends born with a sliver spoon and having the luxuries of life on their finger-tips. You, on the other hand, have to struggle for daily expenses. Feels terrible? But why should it feel so? It's your reality. Accept it! There are failed ones even in rich families. Look around and you will find many who had an even worse family background than yours. They have proven their mettle and got all that they were looking for. If you get success despite coming from an impoverished background, it tastes even better. For a rich man who has seen opulence since childhood days, wealth may not matter and he may still be unhappy for some other reasons. As you know, the wheel of life contains eight spokes and money is just one of them. Even a rich man can be unhappy for health, relationship or security reasons and an average to wealthy person could be joyful on the journey he has been through.

If you look at any extra-ordinary success story, you will realize very soon that 'perspective' has played a pivotal role. When a businessman makes the company bigger, he is looking at every rejection as an opportunity to try a new avenue; he perceives every threat from opponents as a validation of the disruptive power of his business idea. Every roadblock gives a trigger and conviction to do things afresh. Every rejection gives a renewed assurance that the path is right, as otherwise the road would not have been so tough. Easy outcomes need easy efforts, and great outcomes need great efforts. Every little resource comes out as a big means to success. Every little success becomes a moment of celebration. Also, the very realisation that for every ten people who do not support your idea, there are at least two who are going gaga over the success of your idea and will do everything possible to help you grow is good enough to keep pumping their spirits. This is how a long road to success becomes an enjoyable journey.

Having the right perspective is necessary for your success.

Reflect over the ideas expressed in this chapter carefully. It will do great good to your aim to be a successful person.

The four different forms of mindset about which I have written a lot in many of my books are as follows:

- ⊙ Winning Mindset
- ⊙ Learning Mindset
- ⊙ Positive Mindset
- ⊙ Money Mindset

I hope you have a strong feeling of **winning mindset.** This perspective drives you to see problems as stepping stones to success and greatness. This perspective allows you to see obstacles as opportunities.

## Learning Mindset

Learning mindset is a way of thinking which just a few people develop. They make learning a lifelong habit. They learn from books, people, experiences, videos, teachers, students, family members and everyone and everything. They do not stop learning after graduating from college. The world becomes their learning ground.

If you keenly observe the writings of some of the wisest people like Kabir Das and Rahim, you will find that they give most of their examples from nature and life. Kabir has written about some of the most powerful lessons derived from lakes, ponds, rivers, sea and trees. You can actually get all the necessary lessons from your surrounding if you develop the mindset of a learner.

One of the simplest ways to develop this type of mindset is to sit in meditation every day in the morning and contemplate about the learnings which you got from your surrounding in the last twenty-four hours. Let me give some example of how you can learn even from an unpleasant experience:

**You got late for the office and spent all day feeling bad for the lack of your discipline.**

This has a deep-rooted message from the Universe. You need to train your brain to be more disciplined. But how to do that? Let me share a simple, but workable way and this can be practised in all walks of life. You need to see the following two pictures in your mind very clearly:

First, see the picture of you reaching the office before time every day and being able to do a good amount of quality work even before people start entering the office. You have planned your day and fixed the priorities for the day. Since you have blocked your day, others will not penetrate into your day and make you do things that are important for them and not for you. You have become the master of your day. You are going to reign your day better, and that will make you a true 'emperor of your destiny' as your day defines your weeks, your weeks define your months, and your months define your years. And as you all know, your years become your life and destiny.

Second, see the picture of you getting late and getting a call from your manager for something you should have done and emailed first thing in the morning. You got late, and in the process forgot to see the email. Now you are in trouble and get a stern feedback from the superior who was supposed to update the board on this important topic today morning. Your entire day and week suffer because of you beginning one day late.

Life is all about pain and pleasure. You have to see the 'pleasure of being early' which should be more intense than the 'pain of being late'. This intense picture of pleasure will make you be in the office earlier provided you 'see these pictures' clearly in your mind.

Sometime spared in the morning for meditation is the best to train your brain.

People are also driven by the pain of losing something. Hence, the second picture also plays a very vital role. You want to attain the pleasure of a great day and walk away from the pain of a bad day. Both will make you move in the same direction. These forces do not contradict, but these, buttress each other.

And boom! Here you are reaching the office before time every day. As you start doing this more often, you start realizing the pleasures of being early and the picture of pleasure become stronger and permanent. And it becomes a loop for positivity which takes you to the path of greatness.

Did you just see how beautifully you used two diametrically opposite emotions of 'pain' and 'pleasure' to your advantage? That's why I say – this is a magical world. Come what may, you may turn this to your advantage. All that you need is a winning mindset.

To me, the whole universe is a university which has all the lessons hidden within it. You just have to keep your mind open to receive the messages. The universe is the most powerful transmitter that one can ever design, but is our mind the best receiver of these messages? Often, while the Universe is the best transmitter, our mind is a weak receiver. Most of us have a mind which is like a mobile phone with its 'airplane mode' on.

We are simply not observing and learning from all that we see around us.

## Positive Mindset

Coming to the third type of mindset – always be a positive person and don't let negativity come to you. Always look for beauties which anyway surround you.

The best way to build the mindset of a positive person is to practice 'Attitude of Gratitude' and count ten blessings every day. As you do this every day, you become a person who always looks at the brighter side of life. You see the glass as full – half full with water and half full with air. This is a winning advantage in a world where most of the people see the glass as half empty. If you find it difficult to experience how to build the mindset of a positive person, do the simplest thing – join me in my magical morning rituals for greatness programme about which I have written in other chapters as well. You can join me three days a week at 5:30 a.m. in which you will practice many rituals or habits, including the attitude of gratitude.

## Money Mindset

Your life is like a 'car', your vision is the 'destination' and the fuel in the car is 'money' in your bank or pocket. Without money, nothing moves. You need money for food, clothing, travelling, hosting customers over a dinner, marrying, and bearing the cost of education of your children. You need money to travel around the world or fulfil your dreams and passions. You need money to get the right medical treatment for your family members. You can use the extra money that you have to contribute to the society and make others' life better and happier.

Money is the 'fuel' which keeps the 'car' of your life going.

Still, while driving, you are excited to think of the destination and not the fuel in the car. Nobody says, "Wow, I have got my fuel tank full. What an exciting feeling it is!" People do feel excited about their destination and the places they want to visit. That is where the fun lies. They never feel excited about having fuel in the tank. Without money, you can't move an inch, but the real fun comes from having the vision in life.

Apart from wealth, what is equally important is health and joys. I always advise my mentees who join me for one-to-one coaching (check www.coachauthorarun.com to know more about coaching) to set their goals of life along the wheel of life, which includes eight spokes with money being one spoke and an important one at that. Other spokes include career, self-development, health, fun and recreation, family, social relationships, passion and contribution to the society.

Now, focussing on this rather unconventional type of mindset, money needs to be managed right since an early age. You must build the habit of saving a part of your monthly earning, regularly. Drop by drop, an ocean is built, and this is true in money management, too. If you just keep a little part of your income aside every month, you will see a good sum being created over the next few years.

If you are a student, you must be getting some money every month from your parents. Treat this as your 'monthly earning' and apply the same principle here as well. Save some money every month and don't just keep the money in fixed deposits. Instead, invest it in SIPs to get a good return. You will see your money getting almost doubled in 6-7 years. This money will support you with your future education, skill building and self-development, apart from seeing you through your 'runway time' during which you prepare for the flight of your dreams to take off.

You should also know how to create your own financial goals. Set goals on year on year basis.

If needed, take up a financial course and there are many low-cost courses available on Udemy and other platforms.

I remember, during one of my visits to Jaipur, I happened to speak with a Marwari gentleman from a highly respected business family. We spent quite some time together as it was the eve of Diwali and we went to gift sweet packets to some under privileged people. Then we had lunch together and I asked him a question after seeking his permission – "What makes Marwaris so rich and successful?"

He said a few things including the money management secret of Marwaris and this is something I would like to share with you. He said that Marwaris spend 25% of their monthly income and save 25% for future needs. They contribute 25% to charity and reinvest the last 25% of their monthly earning into their business to grow it further.

This is interesting. Many people can't even save 5% of their monthly income and he is talking about saving 25%! I could easily connect this with a few of my friends and acquaintances who are doing pretty good financially and all these people had one habit in common – they all save a significant chunk and invest this in SIPs etc. to see it growing. At the same time, majority of people don't even save 2-3% of their income and in the absence of any recurring savings target, they keep buying unnecessary things and don't even know where the money is going!

Wealth management – you must build a habit for it pretty early and keep this habit for a lifetime. You will thank me for this advice. When I was young, there was nobody to guide me. Hence, I am including a chapter in this book on wealth management. This one habit will see you fulfilling your major goals in a proactive manner.

# Chapter 4

## Who am I?
## A question worth answering

If you are a student or first-time jobber, you are at the right stage in your life to start working in the field of your dreams. I have a deep personal experience of the fact that majority of people end up being in the field which may not be the area of their true calling. Their true strengths might lie somewhere else. However, over the last many decades, the society has created some commonly accepted norms about what should be the best career for someone. My father wanted me to become an engineer. In early 1980s and 1990s, engineering, medical, Civil Service and law were a few distinct professions which most of the parents had thought for their children. I used to see every student aiming to make a career in one of these fields. I do not remember having come across any parent who was thinking of making their child a writer, explorer, photographer, singer or career counsellor. These professions did not attract good money and respect.

Now, think of a student who loved teaching. What resistance he must have faced during his childhood days from all sections of the society while choosing his career! Parents and neighbours must have been forcing him or her to choose one of the four professions mentioned above. The child, in his or her heart, might be thinking of becoming a teacher. I am sure, such a student would have found it difficult to finally decide on the field of teaching, at least in the initial few days of his life and career. He knew that teaching people and explaining seemingly tough concepts must be coming easy to him. Still, since everyone around him was not speaking of teaching as a career choice, the young man/woman must have been trying his/her best in either of the four fields mentioned above before not getting into any of these and then settling as a teacher – of course after preparing, while still getting resistance from various sections of the society. In many cases, he/she would have settled in some other field which did not have anything to do with the field of teaching.

Many people in this world have such stories to tell. Half their life is gone and the field of teaching is still calling them. They are however, wandering through the maze of life, carrying a deep sense of regret of not being courageous enough to follow their talents and calling. They would surely have been a successful teacher – and a happy one at that – had they chosen and been in the field which was made by god or universe for them.

It is good that we are in the 2020s. Now, the career choices are many, and people are free to choose a career close to their hearts. The options of being a sportsperson, mass communication professional, writer, trainer, photographer, explorer, YouTuber, social media influencer, speaker, motivator, traveller, and just anything that your heart asks you to be are easily available. Still, having a job is a priority for many, unless you come from a business background. But, there is an ever-growing number of people who are pursuing their passion.

Let me tell you a true story from my recent work experience with an eighteen-year-old boy called Tanmay (name changed). Since the age of fourteen years, he got interested in the field of speaking and motivation. It so happened that once his father had taken him to a community get together in Mumbai. Elderly people were sharing their thoughts from the stage one after the other. When his father's turn came, he pushed his son forward to speak something. Tanmay was taken aback, but had no choice. He came on the stage and started speaking. He said something which, as he recalls today, did not make any sense even to him. But people clapped after 7-8 minutes as he did not leave the mic for some time. That was the first time Tanmay had a new realization – Can he build a career as a speaker? Or as a motivational speaker rather. He came back and started practising in front of the mirror and camera. Soon, he started feeling more confident and tried even harder to learn and improve. Whenever he spoke to people, he introduced himself as the youngest motivational speaker in the country. His positive self-talk and self-belief further enhanced his confidence and today he speaks to senior leaders freely, speaks with me pretty often and invites senior industry leaders as a guest for his YouTube talk show.

Of course, Tanmay has to attend school. His heart lies somewhere else and he works early in the morning as well as late in the evening to pursue his passion of becoming one of the best motivational speakers in the country. He is asked by his parents to continue his studies for some time. Tanmay does this, of course half-heartedly, but he keeps reminding himself of his dream. He is in touch with some of the best motivational speakers through his sheer passion and drive, and will soon start working with them. He has already attended the live sessions of some of these motivational speakers and keeps talking to me about his dream of becoming one of them very soon. I know, Tanmay will attain his goal of being in the field of motivational speaking and being a YouTuber.

My first advice to students will be to create their Vision Board. In this exercise, people discover their vision, purpose, passion, strengths and goals. I am going to write in greater detail on this topic, but be sure, this is one exercise which is a must for anyone willing to do something great in life.

After all, if you choose a career in a field that is not your passion, you will not have the energy and conviction to keep working harder day in and day out. Unless you do so, you will never be a person who can inspire others.

Know your passion and build a life and career around it. You can build the tallest of buildings as per your wishes if the foundation is solid and knowing well which soil on which the foundations are built is going to be the best suited.

## Find the right place if you want to build the castle of your dreams.

Let's know a little more about each of the elements of a Vision Board.

**Purpose:** I have studied many international peak performance coaches and have found that they all have lived a life of purpose. Purpose is the guiding light that motivates people to wake up every morning. Purpose can guide life decisions, influence behaviour, shape goals, offer a sense of direction, and create meaning in life. I have found that purpose gives you enormous power and force to overcome any obstacle in life. Purpose makes it so easy for you to make critical life decisions. Purpose is not about *your* selfish benefits, it's about *others*. It's about society and the community around you. Nobody who has done something great in this world has done so without a sense of purpose.

You can try answering a few questions to understand the purpose of your life. This society has many problems. Which problem in the society do you feel the most touched by? Which problem of the society do you feel so deeply about that, given the opportunity, you would like to solve it with all your might?

Let me tell you the story of discovering *my* purpose. I've worked in the business world for over two decades. I've been collaborating closely with numerous corporate and organizational leaders (MDs). I've worked with thousands of people, especially since I started off in HR. I noted that people mostly work out of fear and not out of intrinsic motivation. Since they are working out of fear, they may end up taking wrong decisions. They may be more inclined towards maintaining the 'equilibrium' rather than questioning the status quo to make it better.

In the pursuit of equilibrium, they start living someone else's life. They start losing their *muscle of courage*. They will forget their life goals. Or even if they know what they want to achieve in their life, they will be too scared to express it openly. The majority of people are not aware of their life purpose and goals and are living under a constant veil of fear. They become mediocre in their thought processes and forget their true powers. But the day they accept the challenge to take full accountability for their growth and excellence, they will find all ways and means to attain their life goals. They will get an inspiring coach, develop a company of good people, cultivate powerful habits, and write their goals. They will start changing as a person. The seed of change lies in the mindset, which must be changed before a person actually wants to be great. The realisation that people, once coached and motivated, can actually work at 10x their current potential gave me the purpose of my life – to inspire, coach and transform people through a systematic process. This purpose gave me the power to start my YouTube channel, write my book, conduct webinars and numerous training programmes and develop a digital coaching platform to transform the lives of people from anywhere in the world. I use these extensively to create a positive transformation in the organizations I work with.

That is the power of purpose. It makes you achieve the unthinkable in life. I encourage you to study this subject and write your purpose statement. You can write to me to know more about how to develop your purpose.

**Vision:** You must know the broad vision of your life. What do you want to achieve in your life? Your vision statement must be written in one sentence. Someone may have a vision to start a chain of educational centres in India; someone else may have a vision to establish a 100% digital university. BYJU's founder, Byju Raveendran, has a vision of letting people learn with fun, to truly understand the concepts and ideas, and to promote their creativity. The self-taught founder has a vision to create an industry which will allow students to learn at their pace and on their own, with the help of a state-of-the-art learning app. This vision has made him the newest billionaire in India, with BYJU's being valued at 5.7 billion dollars. He also has a purpose to help students living in the remotest of towns and villages in India to learn with the same ease and quality with which other students in the country in metro cities might be learning. He had made his app free for all during the days of lockdown due to the Covid-19 situation. Byju Raveendran has proven the invincible power of purpose coupled with vision. His business might be struggling at the moment, but his journey so far was not possible without a grand vision. With certain course corrections – and if his intention is right – I am sure he will end up somewhere many can't even dream of. Remember that saying? When you aim for the moon, you will land somewhere in the stars.

**Core Values:** I have seen, many corporates have their own core values, though many of them do not follow them to varying degrees. There are some who do not follow the core values at all, and there are a few who follow them in a very limited way. I have also seen many corporates convert their core values into a set of ideas which look good only on the walls. However, logically so, the best of organisations – the most successful ones – follow core values very sincerely, though the number of such organisations is very small. After all, greatness is not everyone's cup of tea.

Similarly, every individual can also think of the core values that one wants to follow in life. These are a set of principles and values that one will follow at all times, come what may. When I spent some good time thinking about my core values, I noted the following:

- Energy and enthusiasm
- Daily learning and excellence
- Inspire and motivate people to achieve great results

I try my best living these values every day. I will do all that is required to maintain a very high level of energy. This includes following a strict morning ritual, including waking up early, exercising, meditating, writing and reading my goals, practising breathing exercise, etc. I will learn something new every day. I do so by reading, writing, listening, talking to people, observing things of daily use, being with nature, etc. Now, my mind is so focused on being the best at learning and acting upon it that anything that I see or hear gives me some interesting insight. I can create instant videos of lessons which I learn with each day. Life has turned into such a magical world that the whole world appears to me as the 'university of the universe'.

**Strengths:** If you do not think of your strengths and write them on a piece of paper, chances are that the world will never let you know of the same. Most of the people around you will be happy reminding you of your weaknesses. While teaching people how to make their vision board, I always ask them to write their strengths on the same chart paper on which they have written, sketched and painted their purpose, vision and core values.

Writing one's strengths makes him/her think of using them more often in life. If you don't even think of or write your strengths, how will you even think of using them. And if you are not working on strengths, you will never become the best in your life and career. I found that my strengths include high energy level, power to observe and deduce lessons, writing, speaking, making videos and making new friends. I used all of these while coaching and teaching people. I also use this ability to excel in my corporate life.

Take any success story, and you will find that people worked on their strengths. Sachin Tendulkar failed one of his exams, but became world class in the sport he used to love playing and practising. Sachin used his strength of sportsmanship to the best of his ability. If you want to make Arijit Singh fail, just ask him to build a career in dance. He is a singer and that is what he does the best. Always write down your strengths and try to be in the field of your core strengths to build a great life and career. If you find difficulty doing so, do write to me.

**Passion:** I have a passion for writing. You give me your life experience and I can write pages for you in one sitting. You show me a random picture and I can write pages about it. It's very important for us to identify our passion. I think everyone in this world has a seed of passion for different things. All that they are expected to do is to discover the passion and give it some good time and efforts. The seed of passion should come to fruition. Passion is something you end up doing for hours without feeling tired. If you want to be a great success in life, it's important that you give the same hours of the day to the field of your passion. You should not give up despite initial challenges coming your way, which are bound to come if you think of doing something extraordinary. Try writing or painting on a chart the things you feel passionate for. It's an irony that we give up our pursuance of passion so easily and decide to stay with the daily struggles to achieve mediocre goals. It's no surprise that majority of us remain average and mediocre. Give it a try at least whenever you think is the right time. Join a job if you like, but do something to test whether you can build on your passion in the extra time. It will require extra working on weekends or in the morning or late evening hours on week days, but do follow your heart. It will surely make you happy and feel energetic even if you don't choose it as a profession.

**Goals:** It's surprising that while most people plan for things as little as going from one city to another, we do not plan for the most glorious journey we ever undertake, and that is the journey of life. We do not set goals for our lives. I often wonder why people do not write 5–6 goals over different time horizons. You can write goals for 3 months, 6 months, 9 months, 1 year, 3 years, and 5 years' time horizons as a minimum. You can write your life goals in the template of SMARTER which is detailed as follows:

S – Specific, Special, Stretched, Shared
M – Measurable
A – Achievable
R – Realistic
T – Time bound
E – Enjoyable
R – Rewarding

Goal has to be specific and not vague. Instead of writing that "someday I will have a dream villa", it's better to write, "I will have a penthouse with four bedrooms costing INR 2 crore in the city of Bengaluru by 31 December 2022." You can make it more specific by imagining the colour of the walls, design of the living room, etc. Your subconscious mind will identify this goal only when you 'see' the house in vivid details and review the goal every single day. Goals have to be special – common and general goals do not get anyone excited. Goal should have an element of stretch and should not be something which you anyway are going to attain without any significant effort. Goals should be shared with people, at least with a few well-wishers, so that they remind you in case you forget the goal and deadline.

Goal should be measurable. Instead of saying that I will become rich, you should say, 'I will be richer by ₹ 1 crore by 1 Jan 2022.' This way, you can measure it in rupees.

Goals should be achievable. You can't set a goal of travelling to USA in the days of lockdown in the Covid-19 situation. Of course, with no flights being in operation, you cannot travel to the USA till lockdown is lifted and airlines start functioning.

Goals should be time bound and a deadline is a must. Goals should be enjoyable and you should be able to visualise the fun and joy the fulfilment of goals will give you. Goals should be rewarding and you must set a reward for you on the attainment of your goals. Our mind looks for pleasure and we have to use this inherent characteristic of the brain towards the attainment of our goals.

One sample of writing a goal is as follows. This is the way you can write your goal of having your dream home or villa.

*Amazing! Our villa has five bedrooms. Two bedrooms on the ground floor and three on the first floor. There is a large lawn and fountain in the front area. We enjoy our stay. The villa has a barbeque area behind it. There is a swimming pool behind the lawn. My children keep playing outside the villa. Our parents also stay with us and are so happy. I have my personal office and studio in the front lawn. This is equipped with the best of amenities. Thank you god – it's an amazing villa. My luxury cars are parked in the porch. I love walking on the lawn in front of the house. I enjoy the feeling of my feet touching the grass below. I enjoy looking at the water fountain in front of the portico. When I enter the villa, I see my family picture on the wall…*

Make it as vivid as possible. This is important for your mind to make a clear picture and then start driving your actions to make it a reality.

## Applying the Vision Board in real life

Think of Sachin Tendulkar, or for that matter, anyone who has been able to create a wonderful success in life and career. Sachin Tendulkar had a strong sense of purpose to inspire and entertain others. After all, there is a reason why Sachin has lived such a disciplined and inspiring life that all that one can think of while thinking of Sachin Tendulkar is 'cricket'. People went to the extent of calling him the god of cricket. Such a life cannot be possible without a strong sense of purpose.

Sachin also has a passion for cricket. He could play and practise cricket endlessly for hours day after day, every day. Such long hours of hard work cannot be possible unless you are doing something you are truly passionate about.

Sachin also had a goal in life, and that was to become great and attain the heights of success. This goal did not let him do things many of his counterparts must be doing – late-night parties, eating junk, hanging out with friends and gossiping, etc.

If you develop a **purpose** in life in the field of your **passion** and set high **goals**, nothing in this world can stop you from becoming someone who inspires others.

If this field of passion also happens to be a field of demand for the world, you can become super rich as well. That is the reason a cricketer is richer in India than other sportspersons with almost the same degree of success. Compare a cricketer and a footballer and you know the difference we are talking about. Having said that, you can also create a new demand. Despite the world turning digital, Chetan Bhagat and Amish Tripathi have created an unprecedented demand for books even among younger generations, which is supposed to be 'social media savvy and against the habit of reading books'. All the boundaries are in mind and the world is full of stories of people who have created a new demand by creating products and services which even the users had not been asking for or were aware of.

Take a pen and paper, and write down your purpose, passion, goals and whether you can create a demand in the market. This exercise will make you think in a new manner. It may take 2–3 hours, but this exercise will set your mind to a new thought process. Remember, it all begins with the mindset and thought process.

You will find the mention of vision board in the book *The Secret* written by Rhonda Byrne as well as on the website of Christine Kane.

Friends, the world, and all its rewards belong to those who act. Supremely talented people remain mediocre, and those without any gift of gab become champions because of one key difference and that is their ability to take action. One key rule of success in life is to deliver more than which is promised by you or expected by others. From the cover page, you might have imagined that I will be sharing a few secrets of success in life. That was the promise. In reality, I am sharing one additional chapter on the power of action. Enjoy this chapter and always remember – go the extra distance and do some extra.

People do not respect you for doing what is expected; they appreciate receiving something extra. So here is the eighth secret and law of happiness and success.

# Chapter 5

## Coach and Company

You need a coach in your life for self-transformation.

Funny thing is – you won't really agree with me just like I also did not believe in this for a major part of my life so far. I know right coaches are not easily available, but if you get one, you will see major changes in your life.

Jim Rohn has been one of the finest writers and motivational speakers. His life was in total mess till he discovered a coach for himself. His name was John Earm Shoaff. Jim got mentored by Mr Shoaff and saw his life turning upwards to the peak of success.

Later on, Jim mentored people such as Mark Victor Hansen, Everton Edwards, Jack Canfield, Brian Tracy and Todd Smith.

Most crucially, Jim also mentored the superstar motivational speaker of today's times, Anthony Robbins. In his book *Money Master the Game,* he remembers how he spent $35 to attend a three-hour course of Jim Rohn and how that one course proved to be the turning point of Tony's career. "It turned out to be one of the most important investments of my life," reminisces Tony Robbins.

I have personally experienced this in my life. Things started changing only after I had a coach with me. It was not a formal assignment, but just the mere company of a person who had sought awakening in life proved to be pure magic.

This is one of the reasons why I decided to become a coach. I saw an acute shortage of good coaches around and hence I decided to do to many in a structured way what someone did to me in an unstructured way.

I strongly believe in the fact that everyone in this world is like Arjuna, who has a rare talent which is difficult for others to copy. Having said that, everyone is confused and doubtful and needs a Krishna to navigate his/her life in the battlefield that this world truly is.

Hence, you must get a coach in life. You can have a physical or virtual coach.

**A physical coach:** He could be a person from your city whom you can meet once in a while. He could be a person who has created a personal transformation in his life and is known as a wise person who can and has transformed lives around him. He could be a person who is always positive and wants others to grow in life. He could be a person who is not insecure about the growth and success of his deputies. If you look around, you will find a few such people who can help you transform your life forever. A good coach can bring the maximum changes to your life and can be the single reason your life can be transformed forever. This is because a good coach will share with you all the secrets of success in a fraction of the time that he himself might have spent mastering these principles. He must have read many books, watched many videos, written many experiences, spoken in various forums, gotten feedback, and improvised on many occasions. He might have taken years and decades while becoming a person full of wisdom about life. But he will share all this wisdom in just a few days and help you transform your life forever.

**A virtual coach:** Thanks to the person or people who invented internet and the people who made the data plans so cheap. You can have a virtual coach as well. You can find the best coach for you on the internet. You can learn from the coach without the coach coming to know of this ever. You can follow their videos, read their books, listen to their podcasts and have one-to-one webinar-based coaching sessions. It's possible for people living even in the remotest of remote places to get a coach on the internet. Always remember – *the first step of change will not begin with the coach; it will rather begin with the student.* You need to become that student. You ought to take the first step and start looking for a coach. Where there is a will, there is a way. No excuses. The only person who can come in the way of your mega success is you and you only. No man on this planet earth has the power to deter you from your goal of becoming super successful.

Apart from a coach, the company of people which you keep is equally crucial.

Your company is the most crucial aspect of your life. If you are surrounded by negative people, you will feel incapacitated and helpless. Your thought process, mood, emotions and ambitions are all decided by the kind of people you keep company with. It is an irony that millions of people do not know the significance of this and end up living in the company of people who are busy talking about mediocre issues, thinking like a mediocre person, and being mediocre human beings themselves.

I have worked as head of HR and had my own discovery while working with people. I have discovered that the earning of a person will be the average of five people's earnings he is mostly surrounded by. I often used to do this little experiment. I used to take a person and make a list of five people with whom he or she used to hangout the most. Looking at their salary, I used to see that the salary of the person used to be the average of the five people he used to be surrounded by.

My statement is – You earn the average of money earned by five people you spend the maximum time with.

It is fascinating how important the effect of people around you has on your success and happiness. If you want to be happier, surround yourself with individuals who smile and do not whine. If you want to be richer, spend time with people who earn more than your salary. If you want to be more romantic, spend time with people who are romantic by nature. If you want to build a fitter body, start being more around people who are fitness freaks. If you want to build six packs, you need to be with at least a couple of people who have done that.

Now you know why so many people join the art of living programmes. They want to get happier and want the company of people who know and practise 'the art of living' and happiness.

If there is one thing which is going to help you unleash the true power hiding within you – and this could be 100 times more powerful than your current self, or even more – it is your surroundings. Or rather, it shows how you design your surroundings. And you can design your surroundings. Some people call it the company of people. Of course, that is the most important and crucial thing for you to succeed in life. But it does not end there.

You should choose your company carefully.

Think over these – What kind of people you are spending most of your time with? Are they *energy suckers* or *soul lifters*? In one word – Are they *lifters* or *leaners*? A lifter is a person who will elevate your senses and motivation to the next level. A leaner is the person who will lean against you, and will sap your energy. Unfortunately, most of the people whom you meet in your daily life are leaners and not lifters. Hence, it is important that you design your surroundings. Make a list of the people who surround you. How many of these people are inspiring? How many of these people add value to your thinking? How many of these people want you to grow in life and career? If you realize that most of the people surrounding you are not helping you think big and grow in your aspirations and actions, it is high time you take the biggest decision of your life and that is to change the company of people that you keep. You can change your surroundings in many ways and not necessarily only through people around you.

Let me give a few examples of how you can change your company through inanimate objects.

**A book:** A book can be life transforming. You can change your life forever even while reading one paragraph of the book. You can get a life-changing lesson from that one paragraph, take action, implement that learning in your life, and move on as a transformed person. You do not even have to read a full book. If you can't finish a book, read a chapter. If you can't read a chapter, read a page or at least a paragraph. Or else, you can just read a few lines. Watch the video on my YouTube channel in which I have explained how you can transform your life even with the reading of 2.5 lines of a book! A book can transform your surroundings and help you succeed in life.

You can also change your company by being around more of the following:

- A video
- A podcast
- A family member
- A movie clip
- An observation of this world
- Anything and everything you see around you
- Meditation link

# Chapter 6

## Habits

Habits are everything in life.

I experienced complete transformation in my life through the power of habits. I left some old and weak habits and built new and powerful ones. Many books have been written on the power of habits, but I would suggest that first build some good habits and experience the benefits yourself in your life. Einstein said. "The only source of knowledge is experience." I always advise my mentees to implement knowledge in their life before believing in anything I say. All that I say in my videos and write in books are based on my personal experiences. Einstein further said, "You need experience to gain wisdom." I can't agree more. Hence, instead of telling my mentees to read about habits, I conduct a programme in morning hours (explained in pages to follow and also in other chapters) to make them experience the power of habits in their own life.

This is a long, but probably the most powerful chapter in the whole book. It details some of the habits which I have personally experimented with.

Here, let me speak about the king of all-powerful habits and that is the habit of waking up early in the morning; so that I have some time with myself. If you build this one habit, you will automatically build many new and powerful habits, and you will see in the remainder of this chapter how!

I don't know how many people 'know' or 'believe' in the fact that spending an hour early in the morning can enhance the quality of your life and give you a better access and visibility of your career goals. Knowing and believing are two different things altogether. Many people know many things, but believe in none. Hence, I am using the words 'knowing' and 'believing' separately. You, irrespective of who you are, cannot be great or do anything worthwhile if you do not spend some time planning, thinking and calming your nerves, so that you can take better decisions, and do good work everyday. Days become weeks and weeks become months and years, and life is what you do every single day. Hence, your daily rituals are precious assets for you to succeed in life.

You should experience it yourself. Be early every day by an hour and sit in silence or in a state of meditation. It makes you at peace with yourself. I have conducted many sessions in the morning hours and have seen remarkable results in the lives of people. To begin with, just being in a state of silence for some time makes you feel great, as in today's world of distractions, most people are lost in their day's chores and are not able to concentrate their energy and efforts in one direction. Sit in silence – and then also practice meditation – which is not much different from meditation except that there are different forms of meditation available on the net. Do not get confused. Just sit in silence and focus on your breathing. If you want to know about variations of meditation, just read another chapter on meditation in the same book. This is one of the most powerful habits one can ever form. Some other habits which you can build in the early morning hours are as follows:

- Affirmations
- Visualisation
- Exercise
- Reading a few pages of a good book
- Listening to some soothing meditation or instrumental music
- Writing your diary
- Planning for your day
- Last week – Next week (You reflect on the last week and plan for your coming week)
- Breathing exercises (Pranayam)
- Stretching of body joints
- Reading your goals, etc.
- Reflecting on your last week and next week (can do on weekends)

You can also practise more habits. I conduct a programme called '10x Success & Joys through the power of MMRG' which I conduct on every Monday, Wednesday and Friday for an hour during 5:30 – 6:30 a.m. You can join this as in this programme, the focus is always on building some of the most powerful habits, including those mentioned above. They give you a calm mind, a focussed thought process and a life of conviction and consistency in actions. In summary, you become a person who is clear about goals and is on the path to achieve these, come what may.

Some other habits which you can also build are as follows:

YTT: It stands for Yesterday, Today and Tomorrow. What it means is – you write down the key activities which you have done in the last twenty-four hours and are 'important' in nature. Here, we are not talking about mundane or routine activities which you have to do. We are going to write only important activities. For example, going for a run which is important for health, writing a page in our diary, planning for the day, reading a few pages from a good book, having some good family time, doing meditation or working on an important long pending project, etc. This MMRG (Magical Morning Ritual for Greatness) tells us whether we are doing important activities or are just sucked into the routine work. One becomes great while doing important work and not while doing something urgent.

AOL: This stands for Acronym of Life. Everyone should do this exercise, which goes like this: you have to think of your top 4-5 moments of pride when you achieved something worthwhile and got compliments from people. You need to now think of the qualities for which you received these compliments. These qualities are your strengths or special powers which you need to build on. Working in these areas comes naturally to you. Now you write these 5-6 strengths or talents and rearrange them in such a manner that you get a nice acronym while picking the first letter of the strengths. An example could be – my AOL or Acronym of Life is ECCIAT. This stands for Energy, Connecting things, Creativity, Inspiring people, Action (to make people act) and thereby bringing Transformation in their lives. Similarly, you have to work out a nice AOL for you. Now, write AOL in big bold fonts on a card board and keep these displayed on the wall of your house. See this every day in the morning and ask a question to yourself – are you doing something about utilising your powers?

## Affirmations

Now we come to yet another important daily ritual, which you must practise to change your life for the greatest of reasons – the practice of affirmations.

Muhammed Ali said, "It's the repetition of affirmations that leads to belief. Once that belief becomes a deep conviction, things begin to happen."

The world around you might be busy reminding you of your weaknesses. You have to take personal accountability to remind yourself of your strengths. This is the objective behind practicing affirmations. If you do not think of your strengths, you cannot even imagine how to make the best use of the same. You will always be forced to play on your weaknesses.

The process is very simple. Sit in silence preferably in early morning hours and say these words to yourself while *feeling* the words. Here, *feeling* is very important as merely saying the words will not help much. You can write your own affirmations while keeping in mind the following two simple rules:

1. Write simple and short sentences.
2. Always write the words in affirmation and not in negation. For example, write 'I remain calm even in tough situation' rather than writing, 'I never get angry in tough situations.' Another example could be instead of writing 'I never lose', you can write, 'I am a winner.'

Some of the most widely practised affirmations are as follows:

- I am the best
- I am the wisest

- I am the happiest
- I am a champion
- My powers are more than my problems
- I have the divinity within me
- I love people and people love me
- Day by day, in every way, I am becoming better
- Day by day in every way, I am becoming happier
- Day by day in every way, I am becoming wiser
- Day by day in every way, I am becoming stronger
- Day by day in every way, I am becoming richer
- I am attracting joy into my life
- I am attracting happiness into my life
- I am loved by everyone around me
- I am effectively delivering my first talk to an audience of over 1000 people who affirm my message with a standing ovation
- I am confidently checking the balance of my bank account as I make a deposit of Rs 10 lakh
- I am happily seeing a message of Rs 1 crore deposited to my bank account
- I am looking around at the faces of the people I am helping and I am thrilled to know that I have made a difference in their life
- I am feeling relaxed and grateful to be sitting here in Mauritius with my toes buried in the warm sand, feeling the warmth of the sun on my face
- I am celebrating how easily I breathe through strong and healthy lungs

You can see more affirmations on YouTube. Repeat your affirmations three times daily – first thing in the morning, midday and just before you go to sleep. Regular repetition will gently return your focus to manifesting the life of your dreams. Affirmations are a set of words which, if said to yourself every day, will build a strong positive mindset. These are important because not many people will root for you in this world. This is one responsibility you have to keep for yourself. Affirmations change the direction of your thinking instantly. The best time to say affirmations is morning. The best way of writing affirmations is to use as few words as possible.

Florence Shinn said, "You will be a failure, until you impress the subconscious with the conviction that you are a success. This is done by making an affirmation which clicks."

So, are you going to practise affirmations today? Remember, the power lies in action and repetition to make that action a habit. So, repeat this life-changing ritual every day to see the magical results.

## Meditation

Meditation has miraculous powers. It is the way to undertake a journey within you. It again surprises me to note that, while almost the whole world talks about the power of meditation, only a few people practise this daily. Mahatma Gandhi had said, "In the attitude of silence the soul finds the path in clearer light, and what is elusive and deceptive resolves itself into crystal clearness."

You can understand the magic of meditation from this sentence.

Matthew Kelly states in his best-selling book *The Rhythm of Life*, "You can learn more in an hour of silence than you can in a year from a book."

In my childhood days, we had a chapter on Gautam Buddha in one of our school textbooks. I was a good student, but still could not understand the meaning of "Gautama Buddha attaining enlightenment." Mahatma Buddha sitting beneath a banyan tree and all of a sudden getting enlightenment was beyond my comprehension in those days. I asked my teacher about it, but he simply gave it a pass and portrayed it as a 'divine event which could not happen to everyone'.

"Gautam Buddha was an incarnation of god and hence he got enlightenment. You guys don't think of attaining this knowledge and wisdom ever. Just note down what I told you," he said further.

I was left wondering what the actual meaning of enlightenment was till I started building a robust daily morning ritual including the practice of meditation.

Today, I am very close to discovering what it actually was.

Mahatma Buddha was actually in a deep state of meditation for many days and months. He was always thinking about the sufferings of human beings. Why do people grow old? Why do they have disease? Why do they die? All his faculties were alive towards the problems of mankind and he lived in a deep state of meditation in a forest for a long time. He, through the power of focus and meditation, activated the true power of his brain. He started 'seeing' the answers to the problems of humanity in his mind and through his eyes. He had attained enlightenment. Prior to that, he had lived the life as per virtues of living, e.g., courage, compassion, right habits, etc.

That is the power of meditation!

While meditating, I used to get tens of thoughts and ideas. Meditation de-stresses you. If you are not able to have the right sleep, meditation will surely help. Meditation will make you healthier. You will get closer to your life's goals and purpose. The habit of meditation is simply shutting down, closing your eyes, slowing down your breathing and focusing on something which will take your mind off from all kind of distractions. You can also repeat a phrase of affirmation while meditating. You are focusing on one thing so that everything else drops away.

Try to count to ten without having a thought. You will get a thought even before reaching ten. But do not let this stop you from meditating. Gradually, with practice, you will become so much at ease with meditation that it will become one of the best sources of your happiness and joys.

Meditation has the power to solve most of the problems in life. Many scientists have conducted research on various forms of meditation and its life transformational benefits. We can lead a life of happiness, richness and enlightenment by building a habit of meditation every day in the morning. Also known as *dhyana*, this has an impact on all the vital organs of the human body, which include the following:

- Heart rate
- Pulse rate
- Respiration rate
- Skin resistance

The ability of our body at each level goes up. We get the following benefits while practising meditation:

- Our immunity level goes up. As a result, we are better able to fight against diseases.
- Our cholesterol level is maintained below the desired limit.
- It makes the lipid profile normal.

- Our respiration rate goes down.
- Our basal metabolic rate (BMR) comes down which is good for our health and well-being. BMR is the measurement of energy expenditure of a person during physical, emotional and digestive rest over a 24-hour period.
- It also helps with longevity. If you want to live longer, practise meditation.
- It releases de-stressing hormones, i.e., oxytocin and serotonin which make us feel happy. Happiness is at the root of all successes ever achieved by any human being. You would hardly imagine a person having achieved anything great in life while being in a state of depression and sadness.
- Meditation has a positive and effective impact on cerebral cortex, amygdala, prefrontal cortex, lymbic system and various other parts of the brain. Scientists of Wisconsin University have conducted research under the mentoring of Dalai Lama and found that there is secretion of gamma waves, alpha waves and theta waves, which ultimately increase the level of love for life, people and the world.
- It improves our emotional quotient, intelligence quotient and spiritual quotient, thereby increasing mindfulness in all aspects of our life. We develop the ability to have mindful eating, mindful breathing, mindful walking, mindful drinking of water and mindful talking, for example. To summarise, meditation brings mindfulness in all aspects of our life and makes us a more memorable person with greater success, impact and influence on people and our society.

- Meditation leads to great oratory skills. I had personally experienced this. Our left frontal cortex and left inferior frontal gyrus develop a stronger connection, leading to remarkable improvement in our oratory skills. It appears as if Goddess Saraswati has started speaking on our behalf. I have personal experience of this benefit and would like all the readers of this book to be personally benefitted by the practice of meditation. You should experience the advantages of this practice on a personal level.

  It may be mentioned that the patients of paralysis are not able to speak well because of the disconnection between these two parts of the brain.

- Meditation is also known to cure some of the most incurable diseases. Various types of diseases including AIDS have been found to be eased out in patients, using the powers of meditation. Some of the most dangerous immunological diseases get cured in varying degrees as a result of meditation.
- Meditation also cures the 'fear against fears'. We all have certain fears and fear will never do any good to anyone. We can be at our best in any field of our life, only if we are free from fears. Meditation also gets us free from the fears of life.

I am saying from my personal experience – if you start practising meditation, you may be compelled to write a whole book or a chapter or make a video on the magical and life transformational powers of meditation. Meditation allows you to change your life as well as the life of others. Not only you, but your family, friends and colleagues also will start seeing a renewed energy and enthusiasm within you.

Meditation, even if you spare ten minutes every day, will transform your thoughts, memory and personality to make you more successful and happier in life.

There are four stages of meditation as follows, as suggested by Jack Canfield, bestselling author and speaker:

1. **Preparation:** It is the first stage of meditation in which you prepare your mind to focus on one thought or chain of thoughts. This is often done by focusing on the incoming and outgoing breaths. This can be done while focusing on a beam of light or a ball of light energy, which may be imagined passing through one's body and mind. One key thing to keep in mind is to be kind to yourself and not worry if your mind wanders towards various types of thoughts. Meditation is a celebration of life. As life depends on breathing, so does meditation. To me, meditation and life are two sides of the same coin. In the first stage of preparation, a person doing meditation directs his focus in one direction. The best way in which you can attain this state is to first choose a peaceful, open and airy space where you can sit in relaxation. You can also play light meditation music like the chirping of birds or flowing of water or any light instrumental music in the background. You will find many such meditation music clips on YouTube. You begin by focusing on inhalation and exhalation. You take slow, deep, easy, and long breaths. You realise that your breathing has become more meaningful and effective. You are inhaling more oxygen and can feel the calmness descending on you. After a while, you imagine that a ball of white light is entering your body through the bottom of your left foot. This ball of light enters your left

foot and fills your five toes on the left leg. This ball of light then moves to the ankle and then upwards towards your left knee. This white light is healing, divine, pure, and blissful, and is healing your left leg as it fills it up completely. The white light moves up and it goes to the waist. Your entire left leg is full of this light and you feel the purity of it filling you up. This light cures any pain in the leg or back and you can feel the happy and healing feelings. The ball of light moves up to the left side of your abdomen and fills up all organs, thereby healing them also. It moves up and fills the left side of your chest, including your lungs and heart. Then it moves up to the left side of your neck and then to the left side of your brain. The entire left half of your body is full of the white light and you feel the healing touch. The left half of your body is glowing with this divine white light and now this light moves from the left side to the right side of the brain and fills it up. From there, it moves down and fills up the right side of your neck. The light moves further below, and fills up the right side of your chest and from there to the right hand. The white light then moves down to the right side of your abdomen and then to the right side of your waist. It keeps moving further and fills up the right leg. It enters the right knee and from there to the right ankle, right foot and the five toes of the right leg. By now, your entire body is full of this white light. Your entire body is full of the divine blessings and healing light, which drives any impurities away from your body. You can feel the happiness and health spreading through your body. It's such an amazing feeling for you. Let this feeling of your body being healed by the ball of white light sink within you. This is the stage of preparation and now you are ready to awaken your mind with the thoughts of your vision and goals. You now imagine that the white light is vanishing into each cell of your body. You have billions of cells in your body, and this white blissful light is healing each cell in your body making you feel happier and healthier. The healing light has been absorbed by your body, leaving your body rejuvenated like never before.

2. **Repetition:** In this stage, we repeat some of the most powerful sentences about our goals, dreams and vision. We repeat the statements of gratitude. We can say sentences like:
    - Thank you, thank you, thank you! Thank you so much god for my beautiful children who love me and are a source of abundant happiness.
    - Thank you so much god for the beautiful home which keeps me safe and secure against various weather conditions and worldly dangers. Thank you so much for your blessings on this home.
    - Thank you so much god for my ability to read and write as there are millions of people on this earth who cannot read and write. I am blessed with this ability and I have been using and will use this ability to write my thoughts, publish many books and learn and listen, thereby becoming one of the best professionals in my chosen field.
    - Thank you so much god for all the people who love me and support me. Thank you for the community of people who want me to succeed in life. These people are spreading the good work done by me in the society and are important parts of my growing network.

You can repeat many such statements of gratitude.

Then you can visualise the fulfilment of our goals. You imagine that your goals have already come true and are making you feel proud. Your family and people around you are celebrating this special achievement. You visualise the congratulatory messages you are getting on WhatsApp and other social media accounts and how happy you are on the day. You can visualise the finer details of your goals. For example, if your goal is to live in a sprawling bungalow with a large lawn in the front and a fleet of luxury cars in the portico and in the parking, you should imagine these in vivid details. The subconscious mind wants a clear picture of your goals and dreams.

Then you can repeat your affirmations, which we have already discussed elsewhere in this book. These affirmations could be a few sentences like the ones we follow. We have already read about it and hence I won't elaborate on it here. You can see videos on affirmations on YouTube or other social media platforms or you can write your own affirmations based on your monetary, health, and social conditions. Some of the sentences could be as follows:

- I am learning something new in the field of my personal and professional life with each passing day.
- I am the best learner on this planet earth.
- I am the happiest and wisest.
- I love people around me and people around me also love me.
- I love money and money loves me.
- I am the strongest, both physically and mentally.
- I am the most inspiring motivational speaker and coach.
- I attract happiness, wisdom, wealth and goodness in my life effortlessly and easily.

- ⊙ I enjoy the blessings of god and relish the blissful moments.

After repeating the statements of gratitude, goals and affirmations, you can also repeat your intentions. I have written the power of intentions on another page. Intentions have a magical power and I recommend that you watch the movie on *The Power of Intentions* by Wayne Dyer. It will take you more than two hours, but it's totally worth it. It's available on YouTube.

3. **Reception:** Next is the stage of reception in which you spread your arms or just open your palms while keeping them upwards on both your knees and feel like all your goals and affirmations are coming true. You imagine that the blessings from this universe and god are reaching you. You feel that your life is being filled with abundance of joys and blissful moments.
4. **Closure:** This is the last stage in which you raise your hands above your head and rub them together, thereby causing a warm feeling in your palms. You put your palms on your eyes and feel the blessings on your eyes. You repeat this process thrice and each time place your palms on your eyes. You can also put your palms on any other part of your body which might be ailing and needs a healing touch.

This is one of the examples of meditation which I prefer calling as the integrated meditation as this ritual combines the practices of meditation, affirmations, gratitude and reading goals. If you do this one meditation every day, it won't take more than fifteen minutes. You will find transformation in your thought process and the way you behave and act. This will awaken your subconscious mind, thereby cutting distractions and making you focus only on things, which truly matter for your growth, happiness and success.

## Writing your Diary

Writing your diary is one of the simplest yet most rarely followed ritual. I am saying ritual because this should become a part of your daily habits. Writing a diary is the best way for one to have those realizations in life which can transform life forever. Everyday life gives us multiple opportunities to learn and develop as a person and professional. If we do not capture those moments, we will never be able to extract the juices of lessons from those moments which, if not captured, will appear as dry and normal. Let me take an example: You called a friend after many years. He was excited to talk to you. In the course of conversation, he told you about his job and lifestyle which seems to be far better than yours. He seems to have taken big risks in life and has always set bigger goals than what most of the people around us would have set. You had last met him some ten years ago. Since then, he seems to have moved in life at a much faster pace than you have.

If you do not write these moments in your life, you would easily forget the fact that you have been taking lesser or almost no risks in life and have been leading a regular and average lifestyle. You have stopped writing your dreams and goals and have stopped visualizing your goals on regular basis. Eventually, you seem to have become an average human being as a result of you being surrounded by mediocre people. If you write these memoirs in your diary, these thoughts will get deeper in your conscience and chances for you to take some actions to make your life bigger will vanish in thin air.

*What should you write in your diary?*

I suggest that you write three things – first, you must write about the general developments, which you experienced yesterday. A brief story of what you went through since waking up in the morning until you called it a day. This will include the videos you watched on YouTube, friends with whom you spoke, calls which you attended, the kind of working day you had in the office, etc.

Second, and most important of all, you must write at least three statements of gratitude for which you should be thankful to god and destiny. These could be sentences like the following:

- Thank you god for the beautiful family, which supports me even when the world may turn its back towards me. I know for sure that there are millions of people in this world who do not have a family to support them.
- Thank you god for the ability to read, write and speak. I know for sure that there are millions of people in this world who can't speak, read or write and suffer lots of problems in life. I am so blessed to have these abilities, which make my life so beautiful.
- Thank you so much god for those people who have uploaded life transformational learning videos, podcasts and audiobooks by listening to which I can learn new lessons of life and profession, while being at any place at any point of time.
- Thank you so much god for the appreciation which I received from my peers for my fast reply to their queries. Millions are living their life without hearing a word of appreciation.
- Thank you so much god for the delicious food I enjoyed with my family yesterday evening. I know that there are millions of people on planet earth who struggle to get proper food everyday (you can also write about your resolve to do something good for these poor and underprivileged).

- Thank you so much god for the chapter I enjoyed reading from the book yesterday. I learnt new ideas and decided to keep learning something new with each passing day.

Accordingly, you can thank god for the following:

- Childhood friends whose memory brings a smile on your face
- Long distance road trip which brought so many beautiful destinations on your way last year
- The time you spent last week while playing with your children
- The moment of pride while watching your little one performing on the stage in her school's annual concert
- Pure air, which you breathe in, as there are people in this world who are forced to inhale polluted air. Think of people in parts of the world who are forced to inhale impure air.

You can also thank god for inanimate objects, for example your car which you love driving, your chair which supports you and keeps you comfortable while you read or write. Basically, you can thank god for anything good in your life.

The great philosopher Marcus Tullius Cicero said, "Gratitude is not only the greatest of virtues, but the parent of all the others."

Third, you must write at least one lesson which you took from yesterday. The lessons can be learnt from any life experience, which did not go as expected by you. Let me cite an example. These could be written as follows:

- I am working from home nowadays. Yesterday, I got late for the Skype call which was chaired by our MD. I was late by five minutes because of the delay in being connected to the Wi-Fi. I decide to keep my laptop connected to the Wi-Fi at least five minutes before any Skype call is scheduled to start. I take a decision to be ready for any call or meeting at least five minutes before the meeting begins. I will be before time every day for any call or meeting. People should know me as a punctual person.

- I got up late yesterday. This is because I was awake until late in the night and as I was working on office e-mails. Hence, my dinner and sleeping times were delayed. Today, I decide to sleep by 11:00 p.m. so that I can wake up early and join my early morning meditation, affirmation, exercise, pranayam, diary writing and other sessions as per the normal schedule. These early morning habits give me energy and clarity of thought, which make my day better and brighter.
- I lost my cool while asking my daughter to do meditation in the morning. She was lazily sitting on the sofa looking at her mobile screen, and I wanted her to sit in meditation for at least fifteen minutes. I later found that she was actually checking the school course curriculum on her handset. I could have been more persuasive and calmer. From tomorrow, I will help her wake up earlier and do meditation along with me.

Now, you can see how powerful this simple habit of writing your diary could be. You can write your diary in a notebook or you can write this in your laptop also, especially if you are a digital junkie.

Writing a diary allows you to learn something new every day. It allows you to develop the mindset of a positive person, one who always sees positivity and solutions and not problems and challenges. To him, every challenge becomes an opportunity because the person has developed gratitude and an ability of looking for inspiration even in the most adverse conditions.

## Visualisation

"I had shivers down the spine as I came out of my car and stood in front of the stained and rusted old building which looked more like a shooting location of some creepy Bollywood horror movie. I saw heaps of cement around the old and abandoned office and plant saplings which had become concrete after undergoing many monsoons. Had I not been told that it was a cement factory once upon a time, I would never have known. It appeared to be a premise of the old dilapidated buildings which no one frequented over last many years. The company had left a few security guards who were paid just enough to be there and look after the old complex. Salary of 2-3 guards was the only investment which the company management seemed to have made in the last few years." The senior director in the board of a renowned cement manufacturing company said in the course of my interview with him.

I used to conduct a few weekend conversations with senior leaders and achievers to bring their stories of struggles, challenges and success to the masses. In the same series, I was speaking with this senior leader who had worked as the chairman in a few reputed MNCs and was now working in the board of a reputed Indian cement manufacturing company.

He continued, "That was my first visit to the factory which I had been asked to reopen, renovate and make profitable. It seemed to be a herculean task then, but became easy; thanks to this one habit of mine. Many people talk about the power of visualization, but I actually practise it whenever I am put across some challenging assignments. I visualize the end outcome a few times in the initial days. This is what I did in this case also. I envisioned how the office building and factories were going to look like a few months after the renovation. While standing there in front of the site, I visualized where the new structures and facilities would come up and how the staff will be moving around, eating and working at the refurbished site. I visualized the final look and reinforced this whenever I came there in future. Finally, after six months, when the plant was inaugurated for resuming production, I took a picture of the site from the same location where I had stood during my first visit. It looked exactly the same now as envisaged in my mind's eyes. That is the power of visualization. I always ask people to visualise the final outcome before you start working. It always works..." He said with a smiling face while reflecting on the past few months, which I am sure must have been full of challenges, but also with a sense of deep satisfaction.

This was one of the high points of the conversation. I was thinking about the words of my coach, "All that we emotionalise, visualize and verbalise, will actually materialise."

Later, while doing some research on Virat Kohli and working on a book project, I came across a unique winning habit of the ace cricketer.

He said in an interview, "Visualization is everything for me. When I had to go play an overseas tour to Australia or England or something like that, I literally sat down 2-3 months before and I made a decision in my head that I will take their best bowler on...," expressed Virat in one of his interviews. He spoke at length on how the ritual of visualization had been ingrained in his daily life.

It brings him to some of the darkest phases of his career and how he bounced back from those moments. I can well imagine how Virat must have used the magical power of visualization to win over his Australian opponents.

Virat Kohli was sweating it out to get ready for the cricket series in Australia in 2014. He was at the rock bottom of his career and people around him had started ignoring him and writing him off. He had just come out of a terrible series in England, where he had scored just 135 runs in ten innings. The world had started turning lonely, silent, and gloomy.

It was one such morning, few weeks before leaving for Australia.

He started his practice early in the morning. As he began his run while plugging into his favourite music, he 'saw' Mitchell Johnson as he closed his eyes intermittently. He increased the speed on the treadmill. He saw Mitchell running to throw a ball to him. He saw him hitting Mitchell for a blazing boundary using the same blistering pace Mitchell was known for. While running even faster, Virat was visualizing the look of fast and furious Mitchell Johnson feeling unnerved while bowling in front of Virat. Next came Nathan Lyon and again the same ease of playing the off spinner. This time a loft six in the deep cover area. While lifting weights, while running on the treadmill, while cooling down on the gym ball, while doing push ups and while doing squats, Virat was 'seeing' himself make India win against Australians like never before.

True – all that we emotionalise, visualize and vocalise, will actualise.

I strongly recommend the habit of visualization to all youngsters and first-time jobbers. They should visualise the attainment of their goals often, preferably in the early morning hours when there is relative peace and tranquillity. In case some of you are still worried as to how to practise visualisation, the answer is simple. Sit in silence, preferably in the morning hours, and visualise the day when your goal has been accomplished. Visualise it in vivid clarity and 'see a sense of pride' on the face of your near and dear ones to see you achieve the success you were looking for. Visualise the compliments and adulation coming your way. If your goal is to own a villa, envision that you are taking possession of the villa and see it in all its details, including the design of the façade, the layout of staircases and windows and wall hangings, etc. Keep a little smile on your face and 'feel' the happiness and a sense of accomplishment within.

Do this often, a few days in a week, and see how your subconscious mind gets the message, and then drives you to take massive actions.

## Catching a Pattern

This is one habit which I have started following over the last few days and what appeared to be a simple habit earlier has started to appear as one of the most important tools for self-reflection and development. I have been writing one pattern about my personality and behaviour, which is not serving my purpose. This is one behavioural pattern, which hinders my self-development and excellence.

Most of the people on this planet are not learning from their daily work and lives. They are living in this world as if they know everything, and there is nothing more for them to learn. People carry their egos in their pockets and do not want it to be hurt. If they have to learn something from others, their ego may get in the way. The fact is, if you were learning from your mistakes every day, you would soon grow stronger than the majority of people around you. That is simply because while others are busy laughing at others' mistakes and complaining about their shortcomings, you are busy learning and growing with each passing minute. Hence, you are taking responsibility for your self-development while others are not even aware of their development needs.

'Catching a pattern' is one habit which I learnt from my coach. He taught us to do this one ritual every single day. We were supposed to write one sentence about our habits and behaviours, which was getting in the way of our personal and professional growth. Just the mere habit of writing down your negative patterns will make you realize your development targets. Then you also have to write a counter mechanism or 'antidote' for each of these negative patterns.

So, let us take a few examples of 'catching a pattern'.

**A pattern:** I get easily unnerved by the mediocre thinking of people around me.

**Counter action:** I must understand that I am working with people who have a different way of looking at the same thing. While I need to inspire them, I also need to understand where they are coming from. This will improve our empathy level, which in turn will make us a stronger team. One of the actions for me could be to change my company and be surrounded by people who are better than I am.

**A pattern:** I do not control my eating habits and eat junk food at times.

**Counter action:** I will decide to eat vegetables, fruits, dry fruits and healthier home-cooked food to the max. This will make me feel lighter and healthier. A wise person once said, 'we become what we eat'. What it means is that our physical and mental health are determined by our food and eating pattern.

**A pattern:** I take longer in executing things.

**Counter action:** I will start my day one hour earlier than normal time and go through the pending action items. I will also check all emails and reply to the e-mails before the busy day really begins. This will give me time to think and plan so that there is no delay.

Examples could be many, but following this practise every day will give you an opportunity to think about your life patterns and make necessary corrections.

## Exercise

I can go on writing on this subject, which is at the core of human health, wisdom and success. Physical exercise is not only meant for sportspeople, but it is also needed by anyone feeling low, listless, unhealthy, unhappy, insecure, angry, frustrated or depressed.

Now, you must be wondering, I am stretching it a bit too far. Exercise could be linked to health and fitness, but linking it to so many human emotions is a little too much!

No, it is not exaggerated at all. Exercising does this and more to our health and happiness.

## What is exercise?

Exercise is defined as 'a physical activity that is planned, structured, and repetitive for the purpose of conditioning the body'. Exercise consists of cardiovascular conditioning, strength and resistance training and flexibility. Regular physical activity can improve your muscle strength and boost your endurance. Exercise delivers oxygen and nutrients to your tissues and helps your cardiovascular system work more efficiently. And when your heart and lung health improve, you have more energy to tackle your daily chores.

There are multiple benefits of exercise aside from reducing body fat and becoming fitter and healthier. Most importantly, it improves your brain power; it boosts your immune system as exercise secretes dopamine and endorphin. You might have heard of the acronym DOSE, which stands for dopamine, oxytocin, serotonin and endorphin. While your brain releases oxytocin and serotonin as a result of meditation, it also releases dopamine and endorphins as a result of exercise. This process actually helps your brain regenerate new neural cells and pathways. This actually enhances your memory and brain capacity.

Before the year 2000, scientists used to believe that brain cells start decaying and dying after a certain age, and there is nothing that can control the process. Now, scientists have concluded that regular exercise can actually help create new brain cells and help people maintain their memory and thinking patterns active for far longer. Exercise enhances the flow of blood to the brain, thereby making it function better. Oxygen also helps improve memory by increasing the size of the hippocampus, which is the part of the brain responsible for memory. This is one of the most magical benefits of exercising. This slows down the ageing of the brain and protects against degenerative diseases like Alzheimer's disease and mental disorders like schizophrenia.

Exercising enhances your energy, uplifts your mood, improves your confidence, controls health conditions and diseases, is a fun-filled social activity and provides better sleep.

## Write your intentions

You can read a lot of material on the power of your intention. You might have read about the science behind it. All I can say is – your intentions matter the most. All that you see and experience happening around you or within you is happening due to the intentions – your or someone else's. Now it is all a matter of whose intention is more powerful. Let's take some examples:

- You decide to take a break with your family and go to the nearby hill station to spend a few days. You want to relax and enjoy some time with your family. You go there because of the fact that you have intended to do so. Something inside your mind says that you need to take a break and relax for a while. Wherefrom this voice comes? This comes from within you. Once you intend, you reach the place. Many of your friends, who might also be living in the same situation, might not have had the same intention and hence did not achieve the same results.
- You are not a good reader. You like partying around with friends and family and are happy-go-lucky. All of a sudden, life takes a unique turn and you suffer a heartbreak. You loved someone's company, which is denied to you. That someone does not like being with you anymore. You feel the pain and go into a state of sadness. One day, while driving on a busy street, you see the banner of a book – how to be happy again? Since you are sad, you have the intention to feel the same sense of happiness again and you enter the bookstore. You, who had never read a book, have taken a book in your hands after many years. That's a magic. No, simply put, it's the power of your intention, which makes you stop there, enter the bookstore and purchase the book. It's the same intention which made Mahatma Gandhi decide to stay put in South Africa and not to leave the place

after he met his 'Pietermaritzburg moment'. Was he made of some other element? No, all that he had was a very strong sense of intention. He intended that day that 'you have evicted me from the first-class compartment of the train; I will evict you from my country'. Intentions are so strong that they will make you do things, which otherwise you might never had imagined.

- You are not an early riser. You have been trying your best to rise early in the morning and begin your day with some strong and healthy morning practices. You are not able to execute this for many reasons. You like having a great time while watching late-night shows on TV or talking to your family or go out partying late in the evening. Somewhere in your mind, there is a conditioning that one must sleep for seven hours and hence even if you set the alarm clock for early morning, you can't get up. However, you feel your energy level being low throughout the day, you start feeling some health conditions, you feel the sense of 'self-defeat' everyday due to not keeping your words and thoughts. You decide to make it happen. Your intention has become stronger. It's not a surprise that you will wake up early the next day, as now your mind is set for morning rituals.
- You have not been able to give time to your children as they are growing up. You are caught up in your corporate life. The set of your intentions does not include you spending some good time with your children while teaching them, inspiring them and giving them the direction of their life. One day, you realize your children need some good time over a fruitful conversation. Your intention has grown strong that day. Your intention will surely make you spend some quality time with your children. –

Now, coming to action for you which may change your life forever. All that you have to do is to write your intentions, as many as you can. You can write any number of intentions once you decide. You can write 10, 20 or even 100 intentions in one sitting. Do write them down. You will have a very joyous and exciting experience merely while writing your intentions. These intentions could be the following:

I have the intention to:

- Earn a pay check of Rs 5 crores a year
- Take my family for a holiday to Europe (to make it specific rather than thinking about any international destination)
- Have a lavish dinner in the best hotel in the city
- Finish writing my book in the next ten days
- To write five pages of the book every day, the next seven days (two sittings everyday – one in the morning and one in the evening)
- To eat dry fruits and drink fresh juices every day
- To eat food rich in antioxidants
- To purchase a penthouse with four bedrooms
- To purchase my dream car
- To feed a hundred people at least one good meal every month
- To help people develop a winning mindset
- To inspire young minds so that they become great corporate leaders
- To help my wife with her household chores in the days of lockdown
- To ensure that my family is always in a healthy condition
- To ensure that my children are getting the right education and upbringing

- To get 1 lakh subscribers for my YouTube channel by the end of 2020
- To share my thoughts already uploaded on podcast channel with the world
- To cover 1000 students through live webinars
- To develop my own website to make it easy for people to locate me
- To develop my e-learning university with at least 10 life-changing courses
- To conduct YouTube live talks
- To conduct Facebook live talks and events
- To publish my book and make it a bestseller
- To write to a hundred heads of educational institutions to conduct a webinar for their students
- To grow my YouTube channel by getting at least 100 subscribers at the end of every webinars
- To exercise for at least thirty minutes every day
- To practice pranayams, meditation, affirmations and gratitude every day in some form or the other
- To upload ten meditations on my e-learning portal
- To upload ten different affirmations course on my e-learning portal
- To be ready for all my meetings in advance
- To listen to everyone and their ideas
- To talk to all my team members every day, to build a stronger connect
- To make a weekly summary of actions and developments to superiors

- To summarise the key action points at the end of every discussion and keep all actions in one central repository
- To focus on completing all actions which I promised for
- To be kind to self and people

## Pranayam or Breathing Practices

You must have heard many stories of highly accomplished people speaking about the benefits and miracles of practising pranayam (the art of breath control, practised as an aid to concentration and increase the capacity of lungs). I will share an interesting story. While watching a TV interview show, the anchor asked the guest of the day, Govinda about the secret of his energy. Many of the readers may find it interesting to note that at the peak of his career in the mid-1980s, Govinda was inundated with offers to do movies. He was acting in forty-nine movies, simultaneously. The number could have been more had he not rejected the offer of twenty-five other producers. He could not return home for fifteen days at a stretch and used to nap or sleep for a few hours in between the shoot. It was this turn in his life which the interviewer was asking about. Govinda calmly responded, "I do not know why people do not practice pranayam and meditation regularly. Since my childhood days, I used to practice these rituals almost every day. I owe my energy to these two rituals. In fact, even to my surprise, I found that I never got tired of shooting in so many movies at the same time."

I guess many of you will find it amusing to find the connection between the 'dancing and comedy star Govinda' and 'meditation and pranayam!'

Once I did a series of interviews to get to the science of pranayam. The idea was to inspire others to make this ritual a part of their daily life. I ended up uploading three videos on this subject, whereas I had the intention of making just one. You can find these videos on either of my two YouTube channels.

However, I am providing a snapshot of these videos in the paragraphs below.

Such is the magic of pranayam, and I would strongly recommend to all the readers of this book that they make it an integral part of their daily lives. The benefits will be magical. This is one morning ritual which I have always enjoyed ever since I started doing it a year ago. This is one ritual which has the power to bring out the best of the energy that you possess. This ritual has the power to have a magical impact on your immune system, nervous system, respiratory system, cardiovascular system, muscular system, digestive system, and almost all other aspects of life. The aim behind this ritual is to give a wider dimension to 'prana' which is the essence of life. Everyone must do pranayam is all I can say based on my personal experience. The magical thing about Swami Ramdev is that he spread this practice among the masses in a very user-friendly way. Many diseases which had been declared incurable by medical practitioners around the world, were cured using this practice when done on a regular basis. Swami Ramdev from Patanjali has been a pioneer in this field and I have personally known the fact that many people who were turning hopeless after visiting many hospitals across the world got cured after they came in contact with Swami Ramdev, who inspired and trained these people to practice pranayam on a daily basis. I can vouch for this fact based on my personal experience. My father-in-law, Dr Nagendra Neeraj, has been a part of this healing process for so many people. Many people coming from Canada, Britain and the USA were cured after visiting Patanjali.

Pranayam is all about regulating the speed of breathing. We can learn the art of controlling and regulating all the senses of the body if we practice this one ritual every day; preferably in the morning. Pranayam helps recharge all the cells of the body. Our lungs are impacted the most as a result of this life transformational habit. The capacity of our lungs to inhale, hold and exhale air increases, as a result of which each of our cells starts getting more than usual oxygen after we practice this regularly. When a child is born, he is endowed with thirty million breathing cells. By the time a child is 5–7 years of age, the number of such cells increases to 300 million.

Many ailments which are linked to insufficiency of oxygen in a particular organ of the body get healed due to smooth flow of oxygen. Every cell in your body needs oxygen. Any organ which does not get sufficient oxygen will start decaying. We see this phenomenon in the patients of diabetes, bronchitis, COPD and asthma, to name a few. Pranayam cures people of all these ailments. It also leads to some magical activities at the cellular level. Athletes and yogis can increase the capacity of lungs manifold. This has a great impact on the cardiovascular system. Our lungs, hearts, arteries and brain are all impacted positively due to pranayam.

Anulom-vilom, kapalbhanti, bhrastrika and bhramari are four of the most common pranayams which have the power to change your physical and mental set-up. All the organs of the body get vital oxygen and rejuvenation. Anulom-vilom maintains the balance between yin and yang – the positive and negative forces which actually complement each other as per an old Chinese philosophy.

Even a truck load of explosives (gunpowder or dynamite) will need a spark to bring it to life. Our body has unlimited energy and this energy will never be truly realized unless we enliven it. Pranayam plays the same role to awaken the true energy hidden within our body. It has an impact on the neurotransmitters of our brain because of the secretion of beta endorphins, serotonin, oxytocin, gaba and other 'peace-providing' hormones. 'There is no disease which is not healed by pranayam,' I have heard some wise men saying again and again. Of course, you need to take precautions while doing certain pranayams like bhrastrika in case of any medical condition including blood pressure, neck or back pain. However, anulom-vilom pranayam can be practised by anyone.

There are other types of pranayams as well. Suryabhedi is very useful for the patients of asthma. Patients battling cancer or mental illness benefit a lot by doing bhramari, anulom-vilom and other such pranayams. Sheetli and ujjayi pranayams are another set of life transformational practices.

Pranayams are not only aimed at making human beings live for 100 years (as Dr Nagendra Neeraj always says and he backs it up with strong logic), but also to lead these years happily, while being alert mentally and physically. Pranayam also helps us build stronger memory. I have personal experience of the effect of pranayam on memory. I have seen Dr Nagendra Neeraj having a sharp memory and he gives the credit to this and other such practices.

This practice is magical for students as it helps them build their focus and concentration. This also helps them build their ability to plan and organise. This also improves their emotional balance and stability. This makes them focus their energy in the right direction and not get distracted easily. Hence, students must be trained for this practice since their childhood days.

Pranayam is a must for everyone looking for health, happiness and success. Kapalbhanti pranayam can be practised by people even while walking. There is no right age for starting the practice of pranayam and students can start it any time. Pranayams are best done in the morning.

For children, pranayams can also be practised as a matter of fun. You can make kids sit and 'count the number of inhalations and exhalations'. Make them realize the way they are breathing in and taking oxygen in. Make them count the number of exhalations. Make them increase the number of counts with every passing day. You can also ask students to do this practice in groups. In today's times of virtual meetings, you can also make kids do pranayam in groups where various practitioners can join over a video call. The idea is to create an excitement and interest for children. Students can be asked to conduct an experiment before going for any examination. They can be asked to take deep inhalation and exhalation at least 10 minutes before appearing for the examination.

So, are you going to begin the practice from tomorrow morning? You can drop an e-mail and I can help you cultivate this habit. Or else, just watch this video ('Waking Up Early in the Morning and the Science Behind It' on the YouTube channel 'Transformed You' by Arun).

## Some tips on how to build habits?

In many chapters in the book, you might have read a mention of 'habits'. If you want to be a better version of yourself, you need to build some powerful habits in all aspects of life, and not only in the direction of money or career. Let me share a list of powerful habits which you can build in various important aspects of life.

**Health:** Make it a habit to spend forty-five minutes to an hour everyday doing exercise, yoga or simply going for a brisk walk. Build a habit of being early in the morning and spend some time doing exercise in the magical morning hours. Another good habit which you can build is that of eating healthy food instead of junk food form outside. You can also make it a habit to eat the last meal of the day before 8 p.m. every day.

**Career:** Build a habit of learning some new skills to make progress in your career. If you are in corporate, you can join courses on communication skills, interpersonal skills, leadership, or team building. If you are in sales, join courses on customer segmentation, customer relationship building, negotiation skills or key account management. Another habit that you can build to grow your career is to do an assessment of your last week and next week. Every Sunday, you can spend some time taking stock of important tasks which you completed last week and have planned for the next week. I make my mentees practise 'Last Week-Next Week' every weekend. It is important not to miss any important assignments which you had committed in the previous week.

**Money:** Save a certain percentage of your monthly income every month. It should be in double digits and at least 10% of your monthly income. Gradually, you can build a habit of saving up to 25-30 % of your monthly earning, and can see a huge saving corpus getting built.

**Relationships:** You can build a habit of calling a few of your old friends and relatives every weekend. I personally know many people who have a systematic approach to rejuvenating their connections on a regular basis. They build these relationships in a proactive way rather than jumping to people when they are in need. Remember, people would value your association when they see you as a person who keeps in regular touch and brings some value to them. Hence, we are referring to the habit of proactive and systematic process of building deep relationships.

**Fun and Recreation:** Make an annual plan to visit places if you like travelling abroad. Or else, book places to visit your favourite places across the country, or take your family for that five-star holiday in Goa. Whatever fits into your definition of recreation and fun, should be a part of your annual plan. This also requires habit of planning your year and maintaining a calendar.

These are few good habits which will surely fetch you great returns.

But how do you build these habits which will require self-discipline, at least in the initial few weeks? Subsequently, as you start seeing the benefits, you start finding it easy to build these habits later on. What looks difficult early on become easy later on.

The hack to build these habits is to begin small and make it better in phases. For example, if you are a junk food eater, you can make it a habit to eat outside food only twice in a week. Then you can reduce the frequency to one day in the week. Gradually, you will start experiencing health benefits from this habit and will yourself be less tempted to eat junk or unhealthy food.

**Begin it small – that is the secret to build any good habit.**

Another example – if you wake up at 7 in the morning and want to wake up at 5 a.m., it will be difficult and most likely you will fail. What you should do is to start waking up at 6:45 instead of 7 and then go for a walk. You will gradually wake up on your own at 6:30 or even earlier, over the next few weeks as you get to experience the benefits including more time for doing exercise, planning your day, getting ready for the office, walking in the morning breeze, etc.

Be it any good habit, start small and then ramp up. As your mind starts experiencing the benefits, it becomes easy for you to build these habits.

And as I said earlier, first you build good habits and then your habits will build a greater you.

# Chapter 7

# Discipline of taking actions (DOA)

The planet of success is small, I mean it does not have too many people living on it because of one reason. People, for various reasons, neither take enough actions nor work on improving their acts regularly. One has to simply keep working ahead and keep learning based on experiences and knowledge to make it better. Those who take one decision and stay with the decision with consistent actions, win the world.

It's all about the discipline of taking actions, consistently.

Let's take a simple example of Dr Ujjwal Patni. He always makes a recommendation to his audience in many of his videos and talks. His advice is as simple as it follows – he asks the viewers to do two simple tasks every day.

First task is that of '**Self Audit**' which has to be done every day in the evening. Before you go to sleep, do a self-audit by asking yourself two questions. It's very simple – the audit consists of just two questions, but you need to ask these questions every day for the next thirty days. First question is -- What did I do today which I should not have done? And the second question is – What did I do today that I am proud of?

Dr Patni gives a confident assurance that if people just do this simple self-audit for a month, they will experience a remarkable transformation in their life and career.

Now, you will wonder what is so great about this simple habit? Anyone can do this every day before going to sleep. However, the fact is – most of the people will find it extremely difficult, almost impossible to do this for thirty days. This is because people lack consistency. They can do an act for a day, but when it comes to doing the same thing again and again, it needs discipline. The fact is – if you do this self-audit every day for the next thirty days, you will have unprecedented realisations about the good as well as the avoidable acts which you are getting into. It will reinforce your conviction to repeat more of good acts and less of undesired acts.

Coming to the second habit. This is known as the task of '**Setting a Goal everyday**'.

In this task, you have to set a goal every day and achieve it, come what may. You should not miss it, that's the key.

Now, again you will wonder – this is even simpler. Then why on this earth is Dr Patni saying this with so much passion and conviction? The fact is – very few people are living such a conscious life that they will proactively set a goal every day and achieve it before making a green tick mark in front of the task.

What separates an average man from an extra-ordinary one, is the discipline of doing things every day.

So, what about doing these two simple tasks – asking two self-audit questions and setting a goal every day – for a month?

If you can do these two tasks every day for a month, believe me, your confidence will shoot through the roof and you will be on the path of self-improvement, greatness and self-transformation.

And as I said – it's extremely difficult, though it does not appear so.

It's challenging only because as it requires discipline.

## Power of Massive Action:

I had read Newton's first law of motion in my childhood days. It says, "Every object will remain at rest or in uniform motion in a straight line unless compelled to change its state by the action of an external force."

This law applies in our lives every day. Those who are in a state of inaction find it difficult to act. They procrastinate.

And those who are men of action will keep taking actions. The rich become richer and the poor become poorer because of this law of life.

They do not know that action is the seed through which multiple realizations, feedback and reactions happen. If you do not take an action, it's like killing a baby even before it is born. It's only through action that either you learn a lesson you will never forget in life (as you have personally gone through it), or come out a winner and successful person who will inspire others to act and not just think.

And if you want to build a life of success and happiness, you should take 'massive action'. This term was popularised by Grant Cordone in his book *The 10X Rule.*

Taking 'massive action' means making your goal or the act of accomplishing that goal your duty, obligation and responsibility, as explained by Grant. It means taking full ownership of your problems, mistakes and failures, and doing all you possibly can to rectify them. Taking massive action is of course not a one-time thing.

I realized the first seed of change in my life after I started the first massive action, suggested by my mentor. That was my decision to start taking some time for me to think about the purpose and vision of my life, to change my mindset about learning and winning, and build habits to transform my life forever. I remember the day I woke up early and did just four rituals including meditation, pranayam, exercise and listening to an inspiring video (actually, I took five actions as leaving the bed early is the first and biggest of all actions).

These are basic rituals which anyone waking up early in the morning with the intention to have a better day will do. I started feeling the changes in my day from that day onwards. Prior to that day, I used to wake up early, but only on those days when I had an important presentation to be made or had to catch a morning flight. I was reactive. I reacted to an impending 'need or danger'. Now I had started becoming proactive and waking up early even on the days I did not have any urgency to be addressed. That was a major shift and it all happened in my mind.

Changing after the change makes it mandatory for us to change is a reactive change and changing before the change hits us is a proactive change. 'Reactive change' makes us feel disempowered – even if it does so temporarily – and 'proactive change' makes us feel empowered. Proactive change brings us to the driving seat of our life while the reactive change puts us in the passenger's seat.

This one massive action of starting my day early made a long-lasting impact on my life and I could see the world around me changing fast. Waking up early is a habit only a small fraction of population on this planet can build. Studies show that some of the most successful people wake up pretty early. Once I had read about the schedule of Indra Nooyi, the former CEO of PepsiCo, who wakes up at 4:00 a.m. every morning. This is followed by her sports routine, which is important to bring her energy level up, which in turn helps her take some of the most challenging business decisions and discharge her responsibilities well. This raised my interest in the habit of waking up early and I finished many books, videos, podcasts and content available on the internet, only to find some very interesting insights. I also found that Indra Nooyi was not the only one with this habit. Let's look at the following:

- Apple CEO Tim Cook wakes up at 3:45 a.m. every morning to go through e-mails, exercise and grab a coffee before settling in to his work day.
- Dwayne Johnson is already in the gym by 4:00 a.m. to get an edge on the competition.
- Starbucks CEO Howard Schultz gets up at 4:30 a.m. to walk his dogs, exercise, and then he makes coffee to get the day going.
- Jack Dorsey, co-founder and ex-CEO of Twitter and Square, wakes at 5:00 a.m. to meditate, exercise, make coffee and then check in for his workday.
- LinkedIn CEO Jeff Weiner wakes at 5:30 a.m., checks e-mail, reads the news, exercises, meditates and eats breakfast (all before 9:00 a.m.).
- Richard Branson rises with the sun at 5:45 a.m. to exercise and eat an early breakfast before work.

- Gary Vaynerchuk, co-founder and CEO of VaynerMedia, wakes up at 6:00 a.m. every single day and gets his day started by checking his phone, catching up on the news and then exercising.
- Oprah Winfrey usually wakes up (naturally) between 6:00 and 6:20 a.m. and gets her day going by walking the dogs, followed by tea or a cappuccino, exercise, meditation and breakfast.

These are just a few examples and numerous books have been written on the power of waking up early, but actually you do not need any of these examples to build this habit. All that you are supposed to do is to start waking up early in the morning. You will know the magic yourself. Unless you experience this yourself, no amount of preaching or reading will help.

Most of the population on earth, almost more than 90% of them, finds it extremely hard to build this morning ritual. Hence, I call this a 'massive action' and that's why when given a challenge by my coach to take one massive action, I chose this habit.

This one habit did the following to me:

1. It gave me the confidence that I was capable of taking massive actions, which in turn boosted my confidence. If I can do it this time, I can do this in other fields as well.
2. It made each day more vibrant and energetic, and made me inspire more people throughout the day.
3. It made me get my personal time and refocus my energy on my goals every single day. That cut down on distractions from my daily routine.

4. I used to spare some time for my health, both physical and emotional, and that got me more in charge of my day, weeks and months.
5. My family was inspired every day and even my wife had started waking up early and spending some time doing meditation and exercises early in the morning. She also became an advocate of building this powerful habit.

Let me elaborate the term massive action with an illustration. For a person who wants to be a great author and motivational speaker, massive action means taking almost all of the following actions:

1. **Book:** This involves the actions of writing a book, editing it, doing the copywriting, looking for a publisher and finally publishing the book. It needs promotion initiatives as well.
2. **Videos:** This involves taking the steps of learning the art of speaking, recording, editing and uploading. Promoting the video so that it reaches out to more and more people is another step. The idea behind uploading a video is to reach out to larger number of people in the least possible time and promotion is a key requirement here.
3. **Motivational speaking:** You need to have a forum to speak to the audience. One needs to keep practising the art of speaking as one gets better and stronger with each talk.
4. **Facebook and YouTube live sessions:** One has to conduct these sessions to connect with the audience instantly and share one's thoughts and ideas.
5. **Building e-learning modules:** In today's times of social media and internet, building e-Learning coaching and training

modules is a must. These courses can be developed on Udemy, Teachable and other such platforms.

6. **Website:** Even in the times of Facebook and YouTube channels, websites are very important. One needs to have a well-designed and all-encompassing website to act as the central anchor for all other platforms.
7. **Digital coaching and webinars:** In the days of Covid-19, and even before these times, connecting with the audience through webinars is a must. Hence, conducting regular webinars is another must-do for a person wanting to become a motivational speaker and trainer.
8. **Other social media platforms:** One needs to build a good presence on Instagram, Facebook, LinkedIn, Twitter and other social media platforms as well. This requires the discipline of regular feeds and replying to messages of all visitors on the social media pages.
9. **Collaborating with institutions, corporates and charity groups:** It's important to collaborate with various people and institutions to reach out to the target audience.

Massive action is everywhere. This was just an example. Massive action is required for you, whether you are an entrepreneur, corporate player or a farmer. Anyone willing to be great needs to take massive action.

Let's take another example of massive actions needed to be taken by someone who wants to be a world-famous wrestler. We can take the visual example of the movie *Dangal,* which is based on the real-life story of Phogat sisters from Haryana. What are the massive actions the father asked his daughters to take? You will be astonished to see the list even when you might have seen the movie many times. You will find something new and interesting coming out here:

1. Making the children wake up early every day irrespective of what time they went to sleep. This was not easy as they also had to study and do their homework along with other household chores.
2. Going for a long run in and around the village in dark morning hours. Other villagers used to look down upon girls running like boys in a village which had not seen such a sight earlier. This was followed by their study in the school. This means after waking up early and going for a run, they also had to get ready for their school and do their homework. It was surely not easy.
3. To stop eating junk and unhealthy food. They had to build a powerful and heathy body and for this, they had to stop eating anything which made them weaker. This again was not easy as this meant they were now 'different' from their childhood friends who used to be in such unhealthy eating habits.
4. To start eating food which might not be too yummy. Eating rice and rotis was in moderation and eating chicken (without rice) and other food rich in protein was in excess.
5. To practise wrestling every day after they came back from school. This was difficult as they did not have any time to play with other children of the village, which used to be a favourite timepass for them in earlier days.
6. To participate in the battle against boys who were stronger than girls. This was a social taboo for the society to even imagine girls wrestling against boys. It was not only a fight against boys

who were stronger than them, but also a fight against the social norms and established culture. This was the first-time villagers were seeing such a thing happening where girls participated in a sport with boys which required physical contact, a taboo for villagers. But this was the best strategy to boost the confidence of girls and get them ready for bigger battles of life.

7. To leave their home and go to a new city while living all on their own. This was another requirement which other girls from the village were not to bother about. It must have been difficult for a girl to move out of the comfort zone of their house and family home and practise a sport traditionally not meant for girls.
8. In order to be mentally tough and fight confidently and independently inside the ring, they were also made to jump from the bridge into dirty and icy cold water of the river to learn how not to lose spirit when there is none to extend moral support to them.

I am sure you will agree that these were all massive actions, which only a very small fraction of people would be ready to take up. Do you have the courage to fight the 'freedom struggle of your life'? The freedom struggle, which will get you freedom to keep your head high and do the right things. If you want people to love you, you need to do what is right!

Change does not begin unless you take full accountability of your behaviour and actions. Change will not begin unless you understand one simple aspect, 'It's not about them, it's about you.' If you want to change the world around you, you need to change yourself first. The world does not change unless you do. The problem with humanity is that we want to change the world around us without changing ourselves. The world is suffering from the mentality of cribbing and complaining. When we are not happy with someone or something, our first tendency is to change the situation or people around us. That comes easy to our thinking process. We hardly think of changing our mindset.

Let us take a few examples of how the change takes place.

You wanted to have your dream job. You applied for the positions after the advertisement. You prepared for the interview. You were not selected and you were heartbroken. You tried again for the second job and then the third job and then the fourth…nothing happened. You felt devastated. You felt like your world of dreams was ravaged by mishaps and misfortune like the state of Syria destroyed by American bombers. You felt alone and deserted in a dry and parched state in desert, with no drop of water available or visible. You felt like being abandoned in endless Antarctica without any glimpse of food or human soul visible.

Life is the biggest examination at times. An examination which nobody is ready for, as nobody has been taught about how to prepare for this. Life can be the most brutal journey and at times all that you need is the motivation, company and guidance of someone who has already walked on that path. You need the support of someone who already has bled and limped back to life after struggling for years. You need to learn from someone who knows what it means to endure that pain and if you keep walking, the goal is not far ahead.

Life is often like a walk with a limping leg through a dusty and muddy road passing through an endless tunnel, and not knowing if at all the tunnel has any end to it. All that you need to succeed in this journey is to be guided by someone who has already walked on that muddy and dark road earlier. Maybe life is like a tunnel which is long and dark, but there is an end to it. After some tireless walk, the tunnel does open into a beautiful valley which is well lit with the beaming golden rays of sunshine. The person knows that the path is treacherous, but the end of the path is gorgeous. That it would be leading to the valley which has beautiful trees laden with ripe fruits, blooming flowers and scented herbs.

The point here is – you need to know someone who will motivate and inspire you to keep walking and not give up. Life's success stories are written by those who persevere and keep moving. You need to know someone who has already walked through the tunnel and seen the beautiful valley at the end.

*'If you can't fly then run, if you can't run then walk, if you can't walk then crawl, but whatever you do, you have to keep moving forward'.*

*– Martin Luther King, Jr.*

It's not easy for one to keep crawling and moving forward unless one has a person in his/her life person who is better known as a coach or a mentor. One can find many coaches who have been on this life journey.

Going back to the above example, the person who failed in many interviews needs to have a coach who has undergone similar failures in life and knows for sure that these failures are not failures, but are actually lessons to learn from. The most important question is: are we able to learn our lessons? The person in this case has to do some soul searching and be coached to change his mindset, change his habits, change the way he looks at his 'failures' and stay inspired as he knows that at the end of the tunnel is a beautiful valley of life – one which is going to lead him to the fulfilment of all his dreams.

Another example: let's imagine for a while that you are an aspiring entrepreneur who has tried creating a company, but has failed miserably. You have failed with multiple start-ups which could not stand on their feet and succumbed to the onslaught of economic upheavals and competitive environment. You know what it means to tread the difficult path passing through a dark tunnel with no ray of light in sight, and while doing so with 'limping legs' of adversity and scarcity of resources and support system. The chances for your success story will go up multi-fold if you get in touch with a coach who can inspire and guide you. This coach could be a person who has himself tried with many start-ups, failed a few times while becoming a success story that other could grow envious of. Rahul Narvekar, who grew from the impoverished chawls of Mumbai to become a start-up enthusiast having built various business ventures worth Rs. 600 crores. You must visit his website www.rahulnarvekar.com to know the stories of various start-ups which he created. You will also know how he coaches budding start-up enthusiasts. Rahul's website says, "Challenge him with the impossible and he shall do it. Say you cannot do it and he shall make you do it." You can also watch videos of Rahul Narvekar's interviews on YouTube. After all, a person who has been the Director and CEO of Sun and Sands Advisors, Japan, Founder & CEO of The India Network, Director and GP, Scale Ventures Fund, Former Co-Founder, NDTV IndianRoots, and Former Co-Founder of FashionandYou.com, will surely have some pearls of advice which can transform your life forever. Ultimately, it's you who has to take action and move on the path. But all that you often need to succeed in life is a spark which rekindles your otherwise dying spirits.

You can also follow the many life and success stories written by Shweta Modgil who works with Inc.42 and has a penchant for start-ups. She has written the stories of trials, tribulations and success of many people in the start-up domain. Some of these stories will inspire you and will also give insight into the struggle which you are bound to undergo while creating a start-up of your dreams by hiring people who could have been trustworthy. In the process, built a team of like-minded people who think similarly, talk similarly and act similarly. You can bait the person has to take lessons from his 'failures'. He needs to do things differently. He needs to build a team of people who come with a diverse range of talents and abilities. The team members need to have complimentary skills and knowledge so that they succeed as a team.

## Acting Smart

During the years 2016 to 2019, I was working in an MNC in Pune. I was staying in the Western part of Pune and the office was located in the Eastern part. I had to cover a distance of 46km every day one way. By the time I was back home, I would have travelled for close to 100 km every day. It was a long drive and still I was driving through the city only while passing through malls, houses, offices and garden of the large city that Pune truly is. Prior to and after this period, my travel has been pretty much limited to a maximum of 15 km or less one way.

After some initial feeling of losing precious 2.5 hours every day in travel, I asked myself a question – can I use this time to my advantage? Can I turn my adversity of excessive travel time to make my life and work better? Later I wrote many books on how to use the challenges to create a life of fortune for ourselves?

As I started thinking positively, I noticed the following unique points about my daily travel time of 2.5 hours.

1. This time belonged to me. Nobody would bother me in this time knowing well the traffic condition in Pune and the need for safe driving requirements. This was 'me time' and I just needed to find a way to use it appropriately.
2. Considering a five-day-work week, I was getting 12.5 hours every week, which I could have used to learn a new skill or finish 1-2 audio books every week.
3. Since I was driving through the city every day, I could have bought things of family need once or twice a week. I did not have to travel extra during the weekend for those activities.
4. I could have used this time to network. I could have spoken with 4-5 old friends or ex colleagues to reconnect.
5. I could have attended an eLearning course every week to enhance my skills. There are so many courses available on Udemy and other platforms.
6. I could have seen inspiring and skill building videos on the way.

I immediately spoke with a few car chauffeur rental agencies and got a chauffeur for me. I started using this time by converting the rear seat into a temporary learning school on the go. For me, these hours became my 'me only learning time' and soon I became an author, coach and speaker, thanks to the proper usage of this time which otherwise would have gone waste while I sat frustrated in the car.

So, what did I actually do to turn my fortune while utilising one of the most unpleasant moments from my daily routine?

I used the power of technology.

I listened to good audio books using Audible.

I joined live training sessions using Zoom webinars.

I joined eLearning programmes using Udemy and other eLearning platforms.

I connected with my old friends and colleagues using the audio message facility of WhatsApp.

In a nutshell, I used the power of technology to turn my travel time to my transformation time. I became my version 2.0 using this time.

I have written about this in my first book *'My Pietermaritzburg Moment'*.

While conducting digital coaching programmes, I used online versions of creating mind maps to explain my ideas better.

I used the power of cloud space to record and upload all my useful files on Google Drive which I can access from various devices from various places across the world. I do not have to email documents from one device to another or use a pen drive.

Keeping documents on Google Drive makes it easy and neat. You get all documents in neatly named folders in one place. You do not have to worry about which document was kept where. In today's times when people are using multiple devices which typically includes couple of mobile phones, couple of laptops and iPads, etc., it's so easy and relieving to see all the documents on the cloud with the same look and feel on all devices.

When I had to let others know about my programmes, I used to record videos and edit them. Then I used to upload these on my YouTube channels under 'unlisted' category. Then I used to simply send the link with a few lines from me to CHROs and CXOs and many of my clients joined me through this route only.

Again, it's a use of technology.

These are small examples, but the summary is – you need to be technology friendly. Use it to the best. Keep looking around and you will find many innovative uses of new inventions happening around you.

Technology is one of the ways to make you a smart worker and not merely a hard worker.

Human beings are unique among all species as we have unique brains. Hence, while hard work is necessary, do not do the same work again and again for hours without thinking everyday where the same work can be done in a better way or not. Always reflect on what you are doing and how you are doing it and find ways and means to make these better. This is the basic difference between hard work and smart work.

Let's take a few more examples: If you are driving in your own car to a congested market place where you have to spend longer time to park your car rather than doing the actual work for which you have gone there, then it's better to reflect if you should take an Uber or Ola while going to such congested places next time. No worry for parking and you can actually have a lot of time. Smart working requires constant questioning of the status quo, which is rare. That's because most of the people think that they think, but they hardly think and surely whenever they think they think of things they should not be thinking about. So, we hardly think and hence we mostly work hard and work smart.

## Begin small

One of the most important reasons why most of the people fail in life and career is – they want to begin in a massive way and attain quick and big success in a short time. This is not going to happen.

Small good habits when done consistently will give powerful results. Simplest example could be brushing your teeth for two minutes two times a day. Doing so one day will not give you benefits. But doing so consistently for years has kept your teeth protected against decay. It has kept you safe from the horrible trouble that toothache is. It keeps you protected against bad breath, which could be a big problem when you are around people. One little action which takes 1.5-2 minutes, two times a day, has helped you in a big way over the last many decades.

Another example: If you go out for a brisk walk for 30-45 minutes on one day, not much happens, though you will surely feel good during and after the walk. But if you do not do this again, it's as good as no effort put in. But if you keep going out for a brisk walk every day or on at least 5-6 days a week, you will see a remarkable transformation after a few months. You will feel more energetic, leaner and fitter and the changes will be even more visible if you have a good control on your diet.

Moving to yet another example – you feel your English is not up to the mark in various ways. The problems that you face include a poor vocabulary, less fluency in speaking and less confident in voicing your thoughts. So, what do you do? You come across a coach who asks you to do the following:

- Learn three new words in English every day and learn to use them in regular conversation. If you can, keep a dictionary or a '*Word Power made easy*' by Norman Lewis, by your side wherever you go. Make it a part of your daily routine to learn three new words every day.
- Select a topic at random and speak in front of a selfie camera/ mirror for 1-2 minutes on it. Give a speech, record it and watch the video, first without sound and then listen to the sound without looking at the video. First practice will teach you a lot about your body language and the second practice will teach you about your pronunciation.
- Speak whenever you have the opportunity. Speak in front of your family and friends. Continue to speak from the stage on smaller occasions. Your confidence will gradually grow to the point where you can converse effortlessly wherever and whenever.

If you take all the above three actions once and then stop doing it, do you expect much to happen? Almost nothing will change. You will learn three new words and will forget these in no time for lack of practice. You will do some practice of pronouncing words and will leave it for lack of passion and persistence. You will stop practicing the art of speaking.

So, what will change after a few months or years. Nothing! You will keep struggling as a speaker and if this is your attitude towards life, you will struggle in all other aspects including the field of money, career, relations, social responsibilities, passion, contribution to the society, and fun and recreation.

Transformation of life and attainment of our goals is a like sowing a seed and watering it every day. It takes time for the seed to become a sapling and the sapling to become a tree.

Hence, make a small beginning today and do the task regularly. In case you are wondering what to do on a daily basis, let me recommend some of the habits which you can build in your life. This is like a menu card and you can take the liberty to choose few or all of these. These habits will surely take you closer to your goals at the earliest.

1. Write your goals on a time horizon of 3 months, 6 months, 1 year, 5 years, 15 years and 30 years and read them frequently, preferably in the morning hours.
2. Exercise or go for a brisk walk every day or at least on 5-6 days a week for 30-45 minutes.
3. Learn 3-4 new words of a language you want to master and practise them in your daily conversation.
4. Be in the company of people who are better than you.
5. Read a page or a chapter of a book and reflect on the lessons. Try finding a connection between the lessons of the book and your life.
6. Wake up early in the morning so that you have an hour with you before you begin getting ready for the day. Do a ritual called YTT (Yesterday-Today-Tomorrow) in which you think about three important priority tasks which you did yesterday, and the important tasks which you are planning for today

and tomorrow. Keep a log report or journal and maintain the progress on daily basis. Just do this every day for the next few months and see the difference that it brings in your life.

7. Eat a few healthy food items every day. Eating 'an apple a day' will bring good health and keep all the doctors away. Apart from eating fruits, include sprouts and flax seeds and some of these health items in your daily food habits for a great result.
8. Make a list of skills which you possess and the ones you need to build. Join a course and always keep learning something new. You cannot change the educational and financial background you come from, but can surely change the course of your life through daily learning and building new and powerful habits.

The idea is to begin small and take actions. You can also join the programme which I have been conducting every day in the morning hours at 5:30, three days every week ('10x success and joys through the power of MMRG). Just type MMRG in the comment box on one of my social media handles and our team will send you more details to join.

# Chapter 8

# Health

"Arun, I am low on confidence nowadays. I am leading an unhappy life. I am in doubt. I have undergone three surgeries for women centric ailments in the last one year. I have been fed up over the last few months. During our last interaction, you had told me about coaching, but I could not join you earlier. I feel, I should come for one of your coaching programmes," Rama went on in one go as soon as we joined over the Zoom call.

"Thank you, Rama, for joining me over this call today. The funny and ironical thing about this world is – nobody does something in a proactive manner. I mean there are very few who do something about their health in a proactive way. I have sent the messages to you over last few weeks. Then, why did it take you so many weeks to talk to me? Let's thank the pains of life, as in their absence, most of us would not have taken any worthwhile action to make our life bigger and better," I said with a smile and concern on my face. I truly care for my mentees and hence I was happy she spoke with me. Being in the field of human transformation for many years, I know people will bring some change in their thoughts and life if they talk to me even for a few minutes.

The call went on for some time and I was thinking why people take health, and for that matter, anything important in life, for granted so much so that unless they have some serious disruption in health and life, they do not take any action.

A person addicted to smoking will keep smoking ten cigarettes a day – or may be less or more in number – till he can't sleep on a night due to constant coughing and burning sensation in lungs. For the first time now, he is thinking of doing something about this bad habit which he has been trying to shun, but to no avail. Over a last decade or so, he has been smoking despite many people asking him not to do so. But somehow, he is not able to get rid of this habit. Not that he tried. When someone asked, he said with a sense of pride, "What can I do? I want to leave this habit, but the habit does not leave me." And then he would release bubbles of smoke in the air and see them vanishing in thin air.

So, what will happen now that he is awake in the morning after spending a sleepless night? Will he visit a doctor and seek advice? For sure, he will do this. Now he has got a jolt of his life and will be inspired to take actions which actually he should have taken much earlier.

Same is true with Rama. She actually should have come for my coaching programme long back when I met her a few months ago, but she had other priorities in front of her and health or coaching was not one of those. But now, by the time she came, she already had gone through some of the toughest moments on health front.

Why am I telling this story (it's a real one; I have just changed the name to protect identity).

So that you do not take your health for granted.

So that you do not commit the mistake which millions are committing every day.

I am blessed to be married to the daughter of one of the most respected and reputed Naturopathy doctors in the country and have a few health tips for you based on my regular interaction with Dr Nagendra Neeraj. I have had hundreds of interactions on health – rather proactive health management – and have got the essence of the lessons which I learnt from Dr Nagendra Neeraj, Director, Yog Gram, Patanjali.

Here am I sharing the 'must-do' healthy practices for anyone wanting to keep regular visit to doctors away. These are proactive health management practices:

1. Doing some cardio exercise every day. It should be so intense that you should be perspiring. What about 20-30 minutes brisk walk every day, preferably in the morning?
2. Practicing pranayam or breathing exercise for around 20-30 minutes every day.
3. Do some yogasanas every day.
4. Include flax seed (roast, grind, add some salt and take a spoon full either with water or curd) in your meal every day.
5. Include ABCTG juice in your morning intake every day. The acronym stands for the richest sources of vitamins A, B and C i.e. carrots, beetroot and gooseberry along with a hint of turmeric and ginger.
6. Eat home-made food as far as practicable. These foods have the least amount of oil, spices and are fresh. Most importantly, these are made out of love. Health should always be your priority and

not only taste and colour which unfortunately is the primary consideration in restaurant and hotel foods.

7. Have your dinner before 8 p.m.
8. Sleep and wake up early. Ideal time of sleep would be 9:30-10 p.m. and the time of waking up would be 4:30 a.m. Try to get 6-7 hours' sleep daily.
9. Take a slow and leisurely walk before going to sleep. It gives you a good sleep and also helps in digestion.
10. Keep your thoughts positive and keep in the company of people who carry positive energy.

Do as many of these as feasible and build a great health proactively. Doing these on a single day will change almost nothing, but making them a habit will transform everything in your life for the better. You will enjoy the kind of health only 1% of people enjoy.

This is the power of proactive health management, without waiting for things to break down.

I do not want you to become like some athlete or champion. I want you to be the healthiest you can be. Remember, health is a crown on your head only the ailing people can see. A healthy body is like a chariot which will take you to your destinations, provided you take care of it.

# Chapter 9

# Common Issues which bother millennials

## How to overcome the Fear of Public Speaking

"Sir, I would like you to conduct a workshop on a subject we have been debating for some time. We are inducting 1000 – 1500 young students every year in various courses, including Engineering, BBA and MBA. Most of these students come from the remote cities and towns of India. Many of them come to an English-speaking environment for the first time. Since all their life, they have studied in Hindi and other regional languages, they find it difficult to speak in English. Their struggle with language also affects their confidence while studying, asking questions and conversing with teachers. I want the students to be more confident in the art of public speaking. I want them to speak fearlessly from the stage. I want them to win over their fear of public speaking. Can we design a workshop, may be over a timeframe so that the students can learn and practice the art and science of speaking?" Vice Chancellor of a reputed university in the state of Rajasthan was speaking with me over phone.

We had a long conversation after which I designed the curriculum. Under this, I designed the programme in such a manner that the students could first feel their fears and then could practice to win over them one after the other. Finally, they had to speak on the stage, all of them, in the presence of all the faculty members from the university.

I know many students who want to get rid of the fear of speaking and I always ask them to follow these steps:

1. **Selfie Talk:** Choose a topic every day and prepare a speech for 60 seconds. The topics could be anything including 'my college', 'my family, 'my goals in life', 'my country', 'the career of my choice', 'my favourite cuisine', 'my favourite city', 'happiest day of my life', 'three places I love the most', etc. The point here is – you have to push yourself to practice and learn to speak on any topic. Begin with a topic close to your heart. A journey of a thousand miles always starts with one single step and hence a journey of becoming the best public speaker also starts with one single step. First you start with topics which are closest to your heart and then you choose more difficult topics, e.g. 'political system in India', 'how to keep oneself motivated even in challenging situations', 'my vision for my country', etc.

   You have to prepare a brief talk for a minute, to begin with, and then continuously increasing the timeframe to 2,3,5 or more than 5 minutes. You have to deliver the talk to a camera and record the video using selfie camera. Then you should mute the video and see your body language minutely. This will help you understand what works and what does not work for you. Then you have to just hear the audio while not looking at the video. This will help you understand the intonation of your delivery. Selfie talk is the new way of speaking in the mirror/camera.

I would rather suggest that you record a short video everyday for the next ninety days at a stretch. Better still, record one video a day for the next six months or even more as speaking in front of a camera makes you a better public speaker over the course of time.

2. **Talk to the family:** Next action in the series is for you to choose a few family members and ask them to be the audience as you speak on the chosen topic. Please ask them not to laugh at you and listen to your talk as a critique to give you constructive feedback; they shouldn't judge you by your intonation and way of speaking. The very fact that you are doing something which most of the people never think of doing in itself is a matter of appreciation. After all, how many people are actually able to taken the first step or take a new initiative in their life! The world is full of people who keep thinking of doing something important, which even they know will make their life and business bigger, but for somehow they are never able to take any action. This is the single most important reason why most of the people end up living a less than mediocre life. You started with recording a minute clip and now you have started speaking with the audience, even if it's your family members.
3. **Take it outside the family:** Next in the series is for you to talk to people outside your family. You can speak with your colleagues or your friends. Now you are taking the next step of talking in front of the people outside your family. Of course, they should be some of your best and well-wishing friends who would appreciate your efforts and will also give you constructive feedback. They will tell you what is working well

and also things which you need to work on to make it better. A positive and constructive feedback is always crucial for your self-development.

4. **Make it bigger now:** Now, it's time for you to take it to a bigger stage. You start volunteering to give a welcome speech or small talk in your annual festivals or other such events. It could be small, but now you are on the path to become one of the best speakers.
5. **Continuous learning and upgradation:** While taking constantly bigger and bigger actions, you should always keep learning and making it better. Take the criticism sincerely. Always remember that the critical feedbacks are more useful than positive ones. A negative feedback will inspire you to do more and take actions to improve your craft. Continuous upgradation of your craft and to keep moving are the keys to success.
6. **Write everyday:** I am saying this from my personal experience. I wrote many books and as I wrote for many months consistently, I started experiencing a more powerful speaker which was so far hiding within me. I was surprised to see that my power of speaking and having conversations with people increased dramatically to an extent that I could conduct on the spot talks from the stage and conduct interview of senior leaders and achievers without having any scripted questions. I kept wondering about the exact reasons till I did some research and found that the primary reasons were three of my habits as mentioned below:

    a. Writing 1000+ words everyday
    b. Waking up early and doing early morning rituals (I have written in details about this in other chapters), and

c. Recording 700 plus videos

This was interesting as I had never realized earlier that writing every day gives clarity of thought whereas recording videos makes my speaking skills better; waking up early in the morning sharpens the subconscious mind, making us wiser and sharper.

I have designed a workshop while considering these principles and steps mentioned above and have done a pilot run. Results are mesmerising. It is working due to its sheer simplicity and alignment with the natural laws of growth and success.

Students are feeling a remarkable transformation in their life.

The steps mentioned here form the basis of learning any new skill. It's all about starting small and to keep upgrading while taking quick and regular actions. Actions are most crucial as unless we keep taking new initiatives, we will not have a deeper realization of life and how things work or do not work. Actions are important to realize and experience life from close quarters and without these, you will have the knowledge of things, but you will never have a deep connection with the laws of success. Also, you will not prosper as it's only actions through which you can make any of dreams real. Anyone who has ever made it big in life and career has done it only through the power of actions.

## How to get my dream job?

Great companies look for the best talent. Are you willing to be that person who will be picked up the 'best companies for work' list? For example, do you want to be hired by a company like Google or Amazon? We all want to have the best of fortune in our life, but how many of us are willing to work hard towards the attainment of our goals? Very few. We live in a world where comfort and convenience come first. Nothing wrong with these and you need to feel comfortable and easy. However, you will realize that whenever you want to attain something great, you will need to put your comfort at stake for a temporary duration. So, talking about the dream company, take out some time going through the company's website and knowing its core values and the qualities it is looking for in its employees. Then reflect on your talents and traits. Are you the person who meet the requirements of the company? If not, where are the gaps? Which new skills do you need to build? Maybe it's a company looking for strong leadership skills, especially for the positions you want to apply for. So, what about building those skills in life? Take up a course and start working on becoming the person the company is looking for. Preparation and practice matter. There will come a day when you will realize your dreams, but unless you are too lucky or you have a strong connection with a senior leader in the company who will be happy to put his reputation at stake (nepotism) and hire you while rejecting better candidates, you will have to follow the rules mentioned in this chapter. Companies need two types of competencies.

1. Standard competencies, which will help you with any company: Examples could be the following. These are the basic skills which one can develop:
    a. Communication
    b. Inter personal
    c. Drive for results
    d. Creativity
    e. Listening skills, etc.

2. Specific competencies which a particular company will look for. Let's take the example of Google which will also want you to have the following qualities:
   a. Openness
   b. Innovation
   c. Smartness with excellence
   d. Hands-on approach
   e. Close, almost a family like connect with people

You can see that Google will not hire you only based on your skills like communication or listening. It will hire you based on your passion for doing something big, your experiences and ability to reflect on things, your ability to think out of the box, etc. In a nutshell, Google knows that building skills is easier, but building perspective and passion is something almost impossible for the majority of people. One has either these intrinsic qualities within or develops these through intense passion and inner reflection. Companies like Google will be on a hunt for these qualities.

You should visit the website of Google and get some authentic information on its core values, hiring process and its belief systems. If there is a gap, you need to reflect and prepare yourself.

## Staying focussed in a world of distractions

This is a world of distractions. We have an ocean of information on the net. It's just a click away. There are videos, blogs, calls, messages, podcasts and audios at our beck and call. When I was growing up in the 1980s, we had only one TV channel which used to broadcast news at the fixed time in the evening and used to show one movie every week. Now we have uncountable news and movie channels vying to grab our attention. There are short reels and clips on our finger tips. We have a host of movies on OTT. I don't have to add to it. I know what I want to share. The world is full of information and you can pick and choose the best piece of information available to you. Due to so many sources of entertainment, information, learning, contributing and adding value, it often gets complicated, especially so if one is not focussed on the task at hand.

If there is one group of people that has to be especially careful not to get distracted and stay focussed, it is students and youngsters joining companies for the first time. They have an undeniable energy to achieve something worthwhile and if they gain focus towards their goals – and for that they have to fix their goals for sure – they can attain far bigger goals than what they would have attained otherwise. But the moot question is – how to stay focussed in a world full of distractions and doubts? So here are a few tips which will surely help the youngsters stay on the path to growth.

The first 'hack' for gaining focus is – to decide life's goals and internalise these in our heart and mind through daily meditation and actions. Before one knows how to focus, it's important to know where to focus. Hence, setting goals on a range of topics is crucial. The best way to set goals is to identify eight different areas including the areas of health, money, career, passion, family, social relationships, family relationships and fun and recreation. On each of these fronts, one has to set multiple goals on different time horizons. For example, you can set goals on the time horizon of 3 months, 6 months, 1 year, 3 years, 5 years and 10 years, or even longer time horizon. Goals have to be written in a specific way by using the present continuous tense language. You have to write the goals while visualizing that you have already attained the goal on the deadline and describing your feelings on the attainment of goals. This way of writing your goals helps your subconscious brain get the message faster and better.

The second hack for gaining focus is to use the power of repetition to feed these goals in your subconscious mind. This can be done by reading the goals, preferably in early morning hours, everyday or frequently on week to week basis. With you doing this for a few days, your subconscious mind will identify these goals. Then you will be motivated to take actions to attain these goals. These actions otherwise are difficult, but with you repeating these goals on a regular basis, you will have your priorities set well.

The third hack for gaining focus is to surround yourself with people who inspire you to attain your goals and do not distract you in different directions. What it means is – you have to get away from people who are more into things which do not correlate with your goals and get closer to people who support you in the pursuit of your dreams. Your company will decide how focussed you would be towards your goals.

The fourth hack to pursue your goals with focus is to monitor the progress and reward you on the achievement of micro goals on the journey. What is means is – break your larger goal into workable smaller steps and keep celebrating as you obtain smaller interim destinations. Keep rewarding yourself and it will be easy for you to keep moving ahead with focus.

## Persistence

Persistence is doing something despite difficulty or delay in achieving success. Merriam-Webster dictionary defines the word as

– "Continued effort to do or achieve something despite difficulties, failure, or opposition."

Cambridge dictionary says – "Continued effort to do or achieve something, even when this is difficult or takes a long time."

My experience in the field of human transformation has taught me a thing against my initial perception when I thought I could transform anyone and everyone. I learnt the message through many coaching, speaking and writing initiatives that success is not for everyone!

Yes!!! It may sound harsh and demotivating, but the fact is – success is not for everyone. It needs a quality of perseverance which is a rare trait or attribute. It's easy for people to have a vision and start doing something. But as the results are not visible, human mind, which is programmed to seek quick results or at least see the tip of the success iceberg, will tend to yield in the wake of delayed or difficult goals.

And this is where most of the youth of today fail on the path to success. In a world where people can't even wait to see a one-minute reel before shifting their focus to another reel, how can they persist when there is no instant gratification?

Persistence needs real solid character. It requires a person to keep going with the flickering flame of faith in the mind when everyone around him is asking him to change the course and join the masses. It's difficult to keep moving without a trace of results in sight when others are taking the easy path to stay mediocre.

I can cite some examples from my life. I required persistence to keep writing till my fifth book reached out to all book stores in the country. Initial four books were available only on Amazon which did not give me much brand value as an author. But finally, the fifth book went across the length and breadth of the country, to all book stores in various cities including Pune, Mumbai, Chennai, Bengaluru, Delhi, Jaipur, Kolkata and other cities, and gave me a huge brand presence as an author whose books were reaching everywhere. Whenever I visited a city, I also visited book stores which were mostly located in malls, and signed a few copies. Then I started sharing videos of these book signing and author's talk sessions and gradually people started to know of me and my work. Books started selling more and more and this gave me my second publishing assignment.

It was all possible because I never gave up my habit of writing at least 1000-2000 words a day. I was working on multiple books, but always wrote on daily basis, even if I did not have any clue whether someday some readers will pick up my books.

You can see the mention of persistence as the single most important quality in the movie *The Founder* which tells the story of Ray Kroc who founded McDonald's chain of restaurants.

## Useful success hacks for first time jobbers

I have been working in corporates for more than twenty-five years. I have seen people succeeding in their career and becoming senior leaders in a short span of time. I have also seen high potential people failing to rise above a certain hierarchy. I have seen senior leaders suffering on health and relationship fronts and those who stayed in the middle level in their career having a great family life. I have seen these people being happy in any permutation and combination of life and have also seen people being sad in the similar situations.

A successful life is a function of many aspects, including talent, qualification, family background, attitude, social skills, etc.

So, in this maze of confusion, how to navigate the ship of life and career is a feeling which made me write this chapter to caution the younger generation. First time jobbers must keep the following in mind in order to see their career growing.

1. **Seek Mentoring:** Please take a serious note of this point – life is full of surprises and unplanned developments. You might have gone to study in your dream college and on the first day, you see a girl and fall in love. So much so that you are blinded in love and lose focus from your studies. One of the many 'beautiful attacks' of life which can actually sniff life out of you. Don't take it lightly. I have seen many lives getting ruined because of this. This is just an example and there could be many surprising twists and turns which will come at various stages in your life. Hence, all that you have read in books will not suffice. You need to get a mentor or coach. Choose a person who is trustworthy and keep in touch. I am not asking you to get a paid mentor. You can be mentored by one of the senior leaders in the organisation you are working in. Or else, get a professional mentor or life coach.
2. **Networking:** It is always comforting to be surrounded by people who are like you. As a first-time joiner, you would be tempted to be around youngsters like you, who gossip about and do average tasks. You should be off the beaten track. Make bridges with senior leaders in the company. I know it will be discomforting to approach seniors, asking them for some time,

but it will help you with life lessons and higher confidence. It's always better to learn from others' mistakes instead of committing them yourself.

3. **Learn and get certified:** Keep taking up new courses and becoming a better version of yourself. It's always good to learn new skills and be ready for better positions with higher salary and benefits. Recruiters value candidates who keep investing for their own growth and keep learning. You will surely have an upper edge in interviews if you make learning a habit for lifetime. Do not only depend on the courses organised for you by the company.
4. **Set career goals and review:** Set your career goals in terms of positions, finances and timeframes and review the progress from time to time. This will not let you settle in your comfort zone in case things stagnate and you do not feel enough challenges in career. In such a case, if you do not remind yourself of your career goals, it's easy to 'fall asleep' and lie behind others in the race. You may love it or hate it, but the fact is – we all are in a race for being the best in our respective fields. You can contribute to the society and care for others, but you can't do even this if you do not be a success in your chosen field and be in the top 1% of people, thereby earning money and reputation in the society. If you set goals, you stay motivated to take up the matter with your seniors and get feedback to work on, unless they feel you should get a raise of promotion.
5. **Keep a watch on your dream companies:** As you put in your best in your current role, keep a watch on the companies you always wanted to work in. Be in touch with some of the college

seniors who might already be working in those companies. Keep a watch on skills which are needed to get into these companies. If you are the best in your chosen field and your skills are required in the new company, chances are high that you will get a call and get through, even if you go through a few failures on the way.

6. **Professionalism at work:** You can either be popular or seek a great career. You can't have both. I have seen people who will take it easy and play it small while being popular among others. Their need for affiliation is high. On the contrary, I have also seen people who will be focussed at work and will not mind saying 'no' to colleagues in case someone just jumps in to their workstation without prior notice. These employees might be hated by a few, but everyone will vouch for their professionalism – once they agree for something, they will deliver it, come what may. Such employees are more likely to rise higher in their career. Their need for achievement is high.
7. **Business ethics:** Always follow certain ethics as a part of your life. These could be summarised as follows:
    a. Be on time in the office. Rather, be before time for the office as well as all meetings.
    b. Be true to your commitments. If you commit a date, stick to it. Always! It helps in building a brand for you.
    c. Be a support to your manager. Stand by him. If you do not like certain aspects of his personality, do not go around and crib. Do your best. Remember, nobody is perfect in this world, including you. Focus on your work – I mean the part of work which belongs to you. If you feel things are crossing the boundary, do speak up, but to the right

person and at the right time. No gossip please. In case things go beyond the extreme, do check for other options. There is no meaning in living a life while compromising at each step.

d. Set your daily goals and keep a track of adherence. Do not keep more than 2-3 key priorities. There will be small acts and work which will come anyway. Do not worry about these. Keep your focus on your daily most important priorities and finish them. Make it a habit. This one habit will take your career to great heights. What normally happens is – in the absence of daily priorities, people get side tracked and lose focus on the priorities which matter the most for their career.

e. On every weekend, do a 'last week-next week' analysis in which you reflect on the important work which you finished in the week gone by and plan for the important tasks which you should finish in the upcoming week.

## Be Selfish

Are you learning or are you merely sharing your knowledge and wisdom with others? Are you helping others grow, but you are not growing in the journey? Are you offering too many programmes for free and are not charging your customers for the value you are adding in their life and the transformation which they are experiencing? Are you a 'nice guy' who is taken for granted by any or everyone?

Be selfish for success and growth. Let me illustrate the point with a few examples before I summarise the point, not to leave any space for confusion.

Suppose you spend time with people who are below you in knowledge and experience. Who is learning – you or them? Be selfish – spend time with people who are more accomplished than you or those who are ahead in the journey than you. You will learn from them. This will explain why highly successful people do not seem to be caring for people who are lower in the hierarchy than them. They know this secret pretty well – they need to be with people even bigger than them so that they learn, not the others.

Suppose you are spending time with people who are less endowed than you in their finances. Who is getting financial wisdom? You or them? It's certainly them as you are looking down and feeling happy that you have attained more than them, but you do not have any idea of the wealth which others, who are bigger than you, are generating. You need to surround yourself with people who are wealthier than you – of course I am speaking about people who generate wealth through the right means.

You should surely enrich those who are lower than you in the hierarchy of learning and wisdom, but that should be as a part of your intention to contribute to the society. Otherwise, you should entirely be with those who are bigger and you will surely uplift your thoughts, success and wealth faster than you think.

Let me give some examples to explain this idea – suppose I give you two books. One is written by an average writer and the other is written by an accomplished writer. Whose book would you read first. Or may only read one book. Which book would it be? I am sure your answer is – the book written by a well accomplished author with a brand name. The other book, which has been written by a lesser known author, despite this being a great book, would not catch your attention. Why? This is only because you are selfish! Yes, you are selfish by nature because you would only choose something for you which you think is more beneficial to you. By nature, people care for their own needs and preferences. This is one of the truths of the world. There are just a few – and the number is hardly any – who actually do things for others' sake.

If we keep this rule aside, being selfish is not a good trait, but it is the best quality when it comes to your own growth and development. Growing emotionally, mindfully and physically is your responsibility, and hence be selfish when it comes to your greatness.

Your selfishness in this field will make you do a lot better for the society around you.

# Chapter 10

## One solution to all problems – MMRG

I know I have spoken about quite a few traits which you can develop – and you must develop – to be a greater version of yourself. These traits will help you attain all that you have been looking for. You might think – I am being too bold, but it's right. Yes. I am absolutely sure of what I am saying. You can attain all that you want in life.

But how can it be so easy? Wouldn't everyone be able to attain all their dreams if it was so easy?

There is a secret why not everyone can attain all their goals.

In his path breaking book, *Think and Grow Rich*, Napoleon Hill spoke about thirty-one reasons about why people fail. The reasons vary from hereditary reasons to lack of commitment to lack of discipline to a bag of other reasons. Most of the people commit one or more of these mistakes in their life.

Let me take a simple example. Most of the people do not have a definite goal. A corporate guy will think of leaving and starting a company of his own every time his boss will treat him badly. And every time his boss will show him the carrot, temporarily may be, he will again think of staying in the corporate. When he sees a possibility of getting higher increment next year, he will think of staying back in the company and when he sees the increments getting elusive, he will think of leaving and doing something on his own. People keep changing their goal posts. They are hardly sure of what they want to attain in their life.

They do not have a definite goal in life.

A definite goal requires a person to spend some time with himself and meditate over the true priorities of life, every day.

Most of the people do not have time to sit in silence and think of their goals. They have a wavering mind. They change priorities everyday, based on their external circumstances. They are fickle minded. They will take path 'A' and will then change it immediately if they see an obstacle on the way ahead. They come back to path 'B' and start afresh. They again face a challenge or obstacle on the way and change their track. Either they come back to path 'A' again or will take a new path 'C' and that is how they spend years while still looking for the 'path of least resistance'.

They forget one thing – anyone who has made it big has done so while facing massive obstacles and putting herculean efforts. Success requires you to pay a price. People want success, but don't want to pay the price. This is impossible.

Here, the point is – people do not have a definite goal. They keep changing their goals as per the ease of attainment or implementation.

Second point – we also spoke about paying the price. One has to get mentally ready to pay the price as without it, nothing is feasible.

Third point – one has to set goals along the wheel of life.

But, what is wheel of life?

It simply means – in order to lead a fulfilling life, you need to work on goals along various spokes i.e. health, career, finances, family, social relations, contribution to the society, passion and fun & recreation.

You will see people having money and no health. You will also see people having wealth and poor health.

You will find people having a job, but not having time for the family. You will also find people who have time for their family, but no job.

You will find people who follow their passion to find happiness, but do not learn selling and marketing skills which are so important for one to turn their passion into business.

So, what are we discussing here? We are discussing why people either set only unidirectional goals and achieve (or fail in this case also) or they set goals along the wheel of life (though such people are just a few) and fail.

I have been doing some work in this field and have discovered that people need to train their subconscious mind for success and change their mindset, to begin with. Then they have to gain focus, conviction and persistence to keep moving ahead. They need to be in the company of inspiring people and have to find a way to keep inspiring themselves so that they do not get distracted.

I, after years of thinking and studies, created such a platform by the name of '10x Success & Joys through the power of MMRG'. This is a digital programme in which people can spend an hour, three times a week, in early morning hours and become the men on a mission of life transformation. The programme is an ongoing one which is conducted from 5:30 – 6:30 a.m. on Monday, Wednesday and Friday. People join the course for various durations, i.e. for 3 months, 6 months, 1 year, etc. It's my lowest ticket programme where people can seek improvement/transformation at a nominal investment. In this programme, I make people implement various MMRGs (which are powerful winning habits) by practising which, one can attain success along all spokes of the wheel of life.

You can join this by checking the relevant link on https://linktr.ee/Coachauthorarun or on www.authorcoacharun.com. You may also send a message to WhatsApp no 9860198168 for knowing more about this programme.

As mentioned, it's an ongoing programme and let me cite a few real success stories of people (with names changed):

**Raman:** He had attended the programme only for a little more than a week. After attending only four sessions, with each session being for an hour, he decided to quit the habit of smoking. The funny thing is – we had not even spoken about the habit of smoking as I never use any negative word or habit while conducting the programme. My goal is to let people realize their inner power while practising certain morning habits and once the inner awakening takes place, people on their own begin to realise what is right and what is wrong. Their ability to appreciate what is right and what is not increases immensely. They develop an unprecedented focus and conviction for their goals. They say affirmations about the attainment of health, wealth, joys and fulfilment. They 'feel' the sentences that they say as a part of affirmations and in doing so, they develop a realisation about the good habits which they must build. Example of a few affirmations are:

- I am the healthiest.
- I am building habits which make me the healthiest.
- I eat healthy and exercise regularly.
- I inspire others to build healthy habits.
- I know that health is real wealth and I act accordingly

As the mentees begin to say these affirmations, they develop realizations about gaps in their life. If repeated regularly, their subconscious mind inspires them to fill these gaps and some of the long pending unhealthy habits change on their own.

A combination of these new set of habits worked in favour of Raman and he shunned bad habits only to build new and good ones.

**Ritwick:** He is a young boy who is not even twenty. He is just out of his teenage and wants to become a motivational speaker. In fact, he wants to be one of the best motivational speakers and has always been telling people that he is the youngest motivational speaker in the country. He has been conducting programmes and interviewing some of the senior most corporate and enterprise professionals. He wanted to meet a motivational speaker of national repute. He joined me in the MMRG programme and practised being in silence, affirmations, visualizations, attitude of gratitude and other such morning rituals. Within a few days, he got a message from the office of the same motivational speaker asking him to come for the meeting. Not only that, he also got to stay in a five-star hotel when he went to meet one of the clients and somehow ended up staying in the hotel – one of the best in the country – which he earlier had never figured out how to do. He was still a student and hence spending money on luxuries is something he had never planned for. He is close to fulfilling few bigger goals and gives full credit to his habit of waking up early in the morning and attending the MMRG programme. Wise men have said it correctly – first you build powerful habits and then the habits build a powerful you.

**Murali:** He was once a victim of both diabetes and depression. These form a lethal combination and can easily bring anyone down in life and career. When Murali came for the programme, he was in a negative state of mind and did not know whether anything in the world could actually pull him out of the appalling state that he was in. But soon, the *brahma muhurta* started working in his favour. He just built the habit of being early in the morning and then the habits started working to make a better and stronger him. Soon, he was not only out of the disease of diabetes, he was also healthier and happier than ever. He was in the peak state of his energy and soon his manager and peers started appreciating his renewed vigour, focus and energy level. Ultimately, he saw his long pending dream come true. He was promoted – the same promotion which was eluding him over ten years, fell in his lap after he worked on himself and transformed himself as a person and professional by building the mindset of a winner and learner, developing new and powerful habits, discovering his vision and purpose in life and setting goals on a time horizon of three months to thirty years. Today, Murali is one of the staunchest followers and supporters of the MMRG programme and keeps inviting his friends, colleagues and some of the family members. Thanks to people like Murali who have taken massive actions to break their comfort zone and take new initiatives while doing hard work, MMRG programme is growing by leaps and bounds with the number of members shooting up with every passing week. True, first you transform yourself and then you end up transforming the world around you. It is surely not the other way, as majority in the world think.

**Saurabh:** He was unhappy with his place of working and wanted to join a new company at a new place. He, however, was stuck among people who were saturated with their life and did not want to do anything new and significant. The place was small and his career was stagnant. He was not able to maintain his energy level and take necessary actions. As I have always insisted upon, the credit of transformation does not lie with the mentor or coach, instead, it always lies with the mentee or the student. But the initial push or trigger of motivation is a must and that is what MMRG gave to Saurabh...

I have added this chapter to give you one clear action item. Just join this in case you are wondering how to change your life in the real sense.

I am sure after reading this chapter, you will know that this book is not only to give you knowledge; rather, it is meant to actually transform your life by enabling you to take concrete actions.

# Chapter 11

## 10 Pitfalls you should guard against

So far, in this book, I have only written about what needs to be done to be successful.

I think, it's also my duty to write down the words of caution for things you should watch out for. Following is a list of ten pitfalls you should be careful about.

1. **You do not check your company:** People fail because they are surrounded by average people who think in a mediocre manner. Your company matters a lot. If needed, shift to a society where you see accomplished people live. When you see industry leaders driving in their BMWs, it will create that much-needed cognitive tension to make you do great things. Success needs discipline and a conscious decision to stay great. This depends a lot on the kind of people you surround yourself with.
2. **You do not review your daily routine:** Discipline is an important criterion for success. Review your routine, set daily goals and put a green tick mark every day to see whether you are making progress or not. If you do not review, it's easy for you to slouch back on the sofa and binge watch your favourite OTT shows instead of working hard on things which are important for your success.

3. **You do not compete:** Wrong are those who say that you should only compete with yourself. If your baseline itself is pretty weak, you will easily be deceived by your brain into thinking that you are making good progress. Your time is limited and you must compete with the best in your field. Set bigger goals compared to what others make and always remember, you are competing against two people – your own self and the best person in the field. This two-pronged competitive approach will make you see faster progress in life.
4. **You take your health for granted:** You simply can't succeed if your biggest ally – and that is your health – is not on your side. Do an audit of healthy habits. Have you done exercise? Have you taken enough water today? Have you eaten some healthy food, i.e. salads, leafy vegetables, sprouts, healthy grains or are you an obsessive junk eater?
5. **You think you have all the time in the world:** People procrastinate as they think there is always a tomorrow. They forget that today is meant to finish certain tasks and tomorrow will be for more and new tasks. You cannot postpone today's tasks to tomorrow.
6. **You are mostly on social media:** This is the biggest trap for distraction. Social media has so much to offer that it's easy for you to spend hours on screen without even realising the amount of time which you are wasting. This habit is also getting you distracted and not letting you focus on most important priorities. Social media comes only after you have earned your social media time after completing your priorities for that half of the day or the day itself. Take breaks and enjoy the leisurely

time, but not before you have earned your social media time.

7. **You do not work smart:** You need to constantly find ways to do the same routine things which you have been doing over the last many months, in a better way. You cannot afford to do something in the same way in which you or others have been doing all these times. Find a new and better way to do and work smartly. Use technology, find a better way and check whether you are becoming more efficient or not.
8. **You do not invest in your growth:** You need to invest in your growth and self-development. Remember – life is not going to give you any significant rewards if you do not become one of the best in your field. For that, continuous learning has to become a way of your life. Join a course to build skills in important areas. Learning is a key to your growth and prosperity.
9. **Develop the mindset of a lifelong learner:** This is different from the point mentioned above. While still quite a few people invest in their growth, very few actually remain a life-long learner. Here we are speaking of developing the mindset of a learner and learn from various resources. You can learn from books, people, life experiences and practically anything that you see around yourself.
10. **You do not build your network:** The number and power of people in your inner circle determines your power. Most of the words given to a man's ability to build community have been given a slightly negative shade, e.g. 'networking' and 'lobbying'. But always look at these words as a precious quality for your success. If your intention is right and you know your product and service is going to help build a better world, you should

not have any hesitation or shame in using the power of people to further your case. The problem in this world is – negative people do lot of it and good people shy away. The fact is – your 'network' is your 'net worth'.

Guard yourself against these pitfalls and I am looking forward to you being 10x successful in your chosen field.

# Chapter 12

# 16 Commandments for Peak Performance

Since the year 2018, when I started taking actions to seek the secrets of how human beings can actually become their best versions, I kept noting down the truths which I discovered beyond any doubt. I tested these in various life situations and also verified these with the experiences of some of the wisest people around.

These are like those catchy dialogues in movies which people remember for long.

In this chapter, I would like to summarize these undeniable secrets of peak performance and success which, if you pay attention to, will serve you in your career and life irrespective of which field you are working in. These are the distillation of all the lessons which I have learnt after conducting research and reflections in my journey of human transformation.

Let me write these sixteen commandments for your ready reference:

1. Unless you change yourself, you cannot change the world around you. It's important to understand as it's easy to try to change

others instead of changing yourself. Hence, people blame, crib and label others in their false pursuit of changing others. The fact is – they should instead change themselves which is in their control, but people do not do so as they are lazy by nature.

2. Those who learn from mistakes and unpleasant moments are the ones who succeed and win the biggest battles.
3. You must have something to offer to others for building networks. For this, you need to make yourself capable of giving value to others. That is the key to building networks, which in turn is crucial for your success.
4. Irrespective of what you do or say, people will judge you or label you. Nobody wants to put in efforts to know your journey. It's easy to label and hence people will do this anyway. Don't pay attention to this and keep taking actions.
5. It's easy to do something once and it's difficult to do the same thing repeatedly. Flashes of brilliance mean nothing and consistency means everything.
6. Unless you act on the learnings, you are wasting your time. Mere attainment of knowledge means nothing. It's through actions alone that you get your goals.
7. We all have limited time everyday. People who win are those who know their priorities. If you are not prioritising 2-3 goals every day, you are not working where it matters.
8. You have to change your daily habits to be a better version of yourself.
9. Nobody wants to receive hard-hitting feedback. They would not mind receiving it only if they know you care for them and it's is for their benefit. Also, only if it is served softly and

with respect after a few good feedbacks. Hence, propose your feedback or suggestion as a soft consideration and let them decide for themselves.

10. People know what is good for them, but still do not do anything, as by nature they are lazy. It requires too much of efforts to break their comfort zone and laziness does not allow them to do anything significant.
11. You can learn a lot from books, people, life situations and places. Developing a learning mindset is the key to success and happiness. Learning gives you empowerment.
12. We all learn through personal experiences. Unless you make others experience the benefits of your products and ideas, your brilliant ideas mean nothing to the world. Telling and showing will not mean anything. The best way of making one experience the goodness of products is to talk to an audience. Hence meeting people is the age-old secret to building better, profitable networks.
13. Learn the art of being in the present moment. This one ability will make you respond better, make better relationships and do better in your life and career. Your future depends on what you do at the present moment. Best way to develop this power is to practice meditation every day.
14. Unless you know how to market and sell your products and services, your talent, products or services are worth the dust on the roadside. *The Monk who sold his Ferrari* was a failure for first three years when it was self-published by Robin Sharma. It became a hit when it was republished by a well-known publisher and then only people knew of Robin Sharma. There

are many great books – better than this book – which are hitherto unknown to people.

15. Sooner you act on an idea, higher are the chances of your success. It is only through timely actions that you bring your ideas to fruition. Unless you see the fruits, you will never internalise the idea. If you delay actions, ideas die.
16. Your thoughts become your destiny. Your thoughts become your words; words become your actions; actions become habits and habits decide your behaviour. Finally, your behaviour decides your destiny.

Above is the essence of my realizations and learnings in life so far. Please go through these once again carefully and try to weigh the words. Unless you experience these yourself, nothing is going to change in your life and world. Hence, act on these one after the other as test cases.

Knowing and believing in these lessons will make you a better leader and team worker. Let me explain how.

You can use point two mentioned above to hold meetings where people can share their stories of failure. One team member can share his/her failure story and others can learn from this. This prevents same mistake occurring again from other team members working in other regions of the country.

You can use point one to observe and correct the habit of people to crib and complain against others. Ask them what they could have done to make the situation better instead of blaming. Make them aware of the human psychology of blaming and not taking personal accountability. Encourage them to act and make a change instead of just passing on the blame.

Use point eleven to listen to people carefully as you can learn a lot from their words, thoughts and experiences. Every person is a walking book and with this awareness you can make more of your interactions with people.

Use point five to set up recurring meetings for the next few weeks if you want to build a habit among people. Making a change happen needs constant reminders and conversations. Repetition of a good deed is necessary for success, but it's difficult for people to be consistent. Hence, understanding of this principle safeguards you against unexpected failures.

Understanding of point sixteen will always act as a guard for you when a negative thought comes to your mind. Always think positive and things will start turning positive. Always think it's possible and then go for any meeting, event, project presentation or assignment with the mindset of achievement and not with doubts. The problem is – people mostly are doubtful and negative. A positive mind will always win in life. Be a man or woman who thinks positive and be a winner in life.

# Chapter 13

## How to stay motivated to be on the move?

Self-improvement or self-transformation to one's version 2.0 is a journey and like all other journeys, it takes time. It's crucial for you to stay inspired to keep taking actions or else you will again roll back to your older self.

It has been more than four years since I have been waking up and practising some of the powerful morning rituals at a time when majority of people are still asleep. I have been doing this everyday, be it Monday or Sunday. I built many powerful new habits which helped me transform to my new version. A set of consistently taken actions (which I now teach people in my coaching sessions) helped me become a person who can write at probably the fastest pace one can ever write a book over a long-time frame. I became a person who can record tens of videos a day and write inspiring blogs on anything that I look around and see. I became an on-the-spot motivational speaker who does not require a topic to be given in advance. You can tell me the topic just before I climb the stage and that would be perfect. I can connect with everyday experiences, things and my interactions with people to bring the wisdom of this world in front of people.

This transformation is a process which takes time and one has to keep taking actions while staying inspired.

It looks simple, but is it easy?

Not at all.

Hundreds of people joined my WhatsApp groups to be a part of '3 times a week' morning sessions (10x Success & Joys through the power of MMRG), but how many of them actually join at real time? Very few. Those who join, they do so every day and those who do not will not be able to turn up even for a day. Most of them might be watching the recordings which I share after the session is over.

So, what makes just a few people so tenacious and successful in their life? The number is small across countries and regions.

It is their ability to keep them on the go. The ability to stay inspired all the time or most of the times. In the absence of this habit, you won't be able to persist and take consistent actions.

Here, I am going to mention a few hacks which will help you to keep moving on the path of self-improvement. You could be in any field, including the field of corporate, sports, arts, leadership, business or studies. The hacks mentioned here are going to apply to all of you.

After all, anyone can become a better version in life provide one is willing to be so.

First things first – you need to visualise your success while sitting in silence for a while every day. It won't take more than five minutes, but visualisation of success which you want to attain is crucial for your success, as that would give you energy to keep moving towards your goals.

If you want to become a motivational speaker, visualize the day when you are speaking from a stage in front of thousands of audiences and are giving them a goosebump experience of transformation and inspiration.

If you want to become a successful entrepreneur, you need to visualize the day when your company has become so successful that some of the top journalists are interviewing you and your interviews are being flashed across news channels.

If you want to be a great sportsperson, visualize the day when you are being awarded as a champion while your family and friends are among those who are cheering you up. Visualize your picture on the cover page of the top sports magazines of the country.

Success is a tough journey and you need to keep yourself inspired to keep moving on. As you keep moving on, you gather precious experience and make corrections in your path ahead. You correct the mistakes in your approach and keep getting better at your craft. One day you shine on the horizon of success like never before and like no one else can.

When I created my third YouTube channel (the first two are 'Transformed You by Arun' and 'The Healthiest You with Dr Neeraj'), I named it 'Stay Inspired with Arun'.

The motto was clear – to give the much-needed inspiration and guidance to people to be men on the go and win over their dreams of life.

These channels are also important as these give you the 'right inspiring company'. The company of people you keep plays a powerful role in your success. When you follow a channel, which has stories of inspiration, you are surrounded by stories of people who succeeded and you change your company through a virtual source. In today's busy life, it may not always be feasible for you to surround yourself with inspiring people, but it's on your finger tips to stay inspired while following some videos which come out every day.

In a nutshell, as mentioned in another chapter, you need to spend some time preferably in the early morning hours with yourself while being in silence and while practising attitude of gratitude, practising affirmations, setting goals for the day, doing some exercise, doing pranayama or breathing exercises and practising some more morning rituals. Just spend an hour and make it a habit. This is the best way to build a mindset of positivity and inspiration.

# Chapter 14

# What is Human Transformation? – A recap

Many youngsters ask me many questions. They have queries, some of which have been mentioned in preceding chapters. People ask me questions on various topics. They have questions related to wealth, health, joys, clarity in life, confidence, freedom from fear, academic excellence, relationships, focus, conviction, vision, goals, etc.

If we have a look at all these queries – and probably even more which are not listed here – it all boils down to life transformation. Let's look at some of these queries which I have come across and enlist them. Then we will see the common pattern in all of these:

- A corporate employee who has not been getting his increments over the last few years on account of poor performance wants to see his career back on track. He is going through a tough emotional phase and the more he thinks of the challenging situation which he has been going through, the more confused and dejected he feels. He is like Arjuna who surely has some talent, but does not know what he has to do to come out of this situation.

- An entrepreneur who has started a new company is struggling to get funds and grow his company. He has got a brilliant idea which he has started working on, but needs more money to grow his business.
- A student who is getting low marks, wants to study harder and get higher marks, but he has to burn the midnight oil and keep his morale high, even when his neighbours and family members are blaming him for his lack of focus on studies.
- A young man who has broken up with someone is feeling low and dejected. He is feeling as if his world is lost and there is nothing left for him in this life.
- A young girl is scared of speaking with strangers and is shy to break ice with them. She will speak with strangers only on a few occasions when there is no other way and even then she will speak only for a few moments and will go back to her cocoon.
- A senior leader in an organisation wants to lead his team towards a common vision and set of goals. He wants to keep his team together and strong. He wants to cascade the values to his team members. But somehow, he is not being seen as a leader who inspires, bonds and galvanises people to attain higher and bigger goals.
- A tea seller, who has been running a small roadside tea stall, in unhappy to see his constant financial troubles over many years, whereas some other tea stalls are making better money. In fact, a few have risen many times over while using the power of social media and collaborations. He wants to enlarge his business base, but does not know how!

- A writer who has some ideas about a book, wants to write his first book. But he does not know how to begin and keep himself motivated to finish the book which he knows is going to take a long time. Also, he does not know how to look for a good publisher who can not only publish the book, but can also promote and market the book in such a manner that it reaches out to a wider readers' base and becomes a bestseller. After all of this is done, he also knows he has to spend good time and energy on marketing the book himself. He may have to give many interviews and visit many places to let people know about his books. It's going to be a tough and long journey and he does not know how to do all of this. Deep down within him, he knows he loves writing, but does not know how the book will shape up.
- An ambitious writer wants to make his books bestsellers. For him promoting books is more important than the joy of writing. He knows he has to spend time and money on marketing and selling efforts, but does not know how and where to make a beginning.
- A young graduate from one of the premier MBA colleges wants to begin a start-up, but that will require him to speak with many people and seek funds before he goes on working hard to make his dreams a reality and create a unicorn. This journey is going to be tough and uphill and he needs to develop discipline to build powerful habits which will see him have higher energy and drive to fulfil his aspirations.
- An employee working in corporate wants to pursue his passion, but does not know how to do so while not disturbing his flow

of income. He has responsibilities to fulfil and does not know where to make a beginning.

- Son of a businessman, who wants to pursue his passion of photography and build his career in this field, is being cajoled by his father to join the family business. He, however, does not want to be in business. His heart, instead, lies elsewhere and he wants to be one of the best photographers in the surrounding. While he is being pestered by his father to join the family business, he does not know how to muster courage to speak up and begin pursuing his dreams. He also does not want to anger his father and make him sad. He is going to require excellent interpersonal communication and persuasion skills, but does not know how to develop these skills.

I can go on adding more cases similar to the ones mentioned above. Nature of all these problems will differ from each other, but now coming to the interesting and almost magical part of this discussion - while problems will vary, there is an 'umbrella solution' for all of these issues.

One set of solutions will work for all these cases because, at the core, all the problems turn out to be a common problem of human transformation.

Yes, in all the above cases, people want to see a change in the way they see things happening in their life or around them.

Interestingly – and this is the common law of this universe - while all these people want to see a change in their situation or surrounding, it will not happen unless they realise one thing which I call as the magical secret of making it big and attaining the goals of your life.

Based on my long, passionate and intense work in the field of human transformation, I can suggest a magical set of seven solutions to all these people facing various issues as enlisted above. This is going to be truly interesting as the solution to all human problems boils down to a set of just seven topics which you are going to read in the forthcoming chapters.

These seven topics which we are going to study in the following chapters are truly life transformational if you implement these in life. Even if you are not able to follow all of these in life, you can begin rolling out at least a few in your daily routine and see the magical results for yourself.

So, without much ado about anything, let's come to the seven secrets of transformation.

Let's begin with the first one.

It is **your mindset**. A person struggles in life and career because he/she does not make some vital changes in the way the person thinks and looks at the world. Unless you change the way you think, you will continue struggling all your life, and that also, without realizing that there is a serious need to change it.

We have already learnt about these in previous chapters in good detail.

The second secret to success in any chosen field of life and career is – **Habits**. First you change your habits and then your habits change you. You might have read this somewhere or might have heard this from someone, but I am not sure how many of you might actually have got it in your head and heart. Chances are – not even 5% of the readers might have actually got it. You need to build some powerful new habits to gain success in life. The best way for you to build some of the most powerful habits in your life is to be a little early in the morning. In fact, I am so passionate about the power of habits for someone's success and joys that I launched a programme in which I want every Indian to join – it's known as MMRG. I conduct this programme every Monday, Wednesday and Friday. While I am writing these lines, I am in Jaipur on the auspicious and heart-warming day of Diwali. It's 24 October 2022. I am on a holiday with my family and still I conducted the programme. Also, what is even more inspiring to me is – many mentees who have been realising the magical power of habits did find time and energy to attend the programme during the dark morning hours in the winters of 2022. We will speak about the power of habits in coming chapter in details. This surely is going to be one of the most detailed chapters as without changing your habits, nothing changes in your life.

The third most important aspect for the transformation in life is the **discovery of your vision.** Yes, most of the people in this world live their entire life without ever coming to know of their vision, purpose, strengths, core values and goals. I conduct a programme 'Create Your Grand Vision Board' in which I inspire and guide the participants (I conduct it digitally to be able to reach out to as many people as feasible) to discover their vision and other related aspects as enlisted above. I really wonder why people do not get time to think of their vision and purpose in life. I wonder how people can live all their life without ever thinking of their core values and strengths! I know many people never having thought of what their true talents are, and whether they have given some dedicated time to this. I know many who are working in the field which does not belong to them. They keep struggling as they still want to be better than those who are actually working in their field of passion and purpose. How can a person who loves wildlife photography and is working in corporates can ever beat another person who loves leading and working in an organisational set up? Hence, it's important for people to understand the basics of success and joys before competing with others and thinking of being the best.

Fourth secret is the **presence of a good coach**. Even if you are missing on other secrets, remember, this one secret, the company of a good coach, can transform your life for ever for the best of reasons.

Fifth secret which one should act on is the **focus on health.** Unless you have a healthy mind and body, how can you ever be a success? It is funny to see people running after career and monetary success without bothering for health and happiness. They earn money to lose health and then they lose their earnings to earn health. It's ironical, but true. It's important that you always do something on daily basis to keep your health in superb condition. Eat healthy, do exercise and avoid any addiction which could be bad for your health.

Sixth most crucial element of success is the **presence of goals** in your life. So many people live their life without ever realising their life, health and career goals.

Last, but not the least, **company of people** which you keep matters a lot. This is the seventh secret or factor behind success. No person has ever succeeded without being in the company of people who inspire as well as teach you. Presence of right people in your life is extremely crucial. Your eco-system defines your destiny. The kind of people you sit with and spend most of your time with decides the way you are going to set your priorities in life, thoughts and acts. If you are in the company of people who deprecate your vision and pollute your mind, you will be wasting most of your energy while countering these negative forces and hence it's important that you be in the company of people who support and guide you in the right direction.

These seven secrets provide you with a powerful recipe for complete transformation of life and attainment of your goals. This concoction of seven factors is bound to give you all that you have been dreaming or thinking about. All other important aspects of life will fall in place automatically.

I am sure by the time you finish the book, you would have travelled a long distance from just knowing the secrets to believing in them and then taking actions on a consistent basis to seek complete transformation in your life. As I always say – it's not about just knowing. It's about knowing (*janana*), then believing (*manana*) and then becoming committed (*thanana*) to take actions. Majority of people know many secrets of life transformation, but do not develop conviction to be in a state of taking actions. Unless you are committed – which by the way is a tough journey – you will not act and hence you will never know the power of that particular knowledge.

Let me cite a couple of examples of why just knowing does not help and one has to believe in the knowledge which one has acquired.

Example one: Many people know that waking up early in the morning is a good idea. I have used a moderate word 'good', but I know it's an amazing idea indeed. It is life transformational. Robin Sharma and Hal Elrod have written best-selling books on this topic. Since our childhood days, we have heard the proverb – 'Early to bed and early to rise, makes a man healthy, wealthy and wise'. In ancient Indian books, many wise men have written chapters on the power of waking up early in the morning. Our parents and teachers have been asking us since our early days in life to build some of the most powerful habits, including the habit of waking up early in the morning. Scientists in western countries have written so much about the alpha state of mind in the early morning hours. Our ancient scriptures have spoken a lot about the power of brahma muhurta which is from two hours before the time of sunrise to the time of sunrise.

Still, how many people can actually build the habit of waking up early? You can look around the society that you live in and I am sure you will find just a few who have this powerful habit which brings health, wealth and wisdom.

Let me cite my personal example. I was married to Divya – the daughter of Dr Neeraj, a world-renowned Naturopathy doctor – in the year 2003. My father-in-law told me so many times about the power of waking up early. He himself has been waking up at 4 a.m. for over last forty-five years. Despite this, I could not make the habit of waking up early for more than fifteen years after getting married. I had this habit in my school days to wake up early and I maintained this habit till I went to live in hostels. Once I went to the hostels, my habits changed to that of sleeping late and waking up late. And then I could not build the habit of waking up early till fifteen years after getting married. And once I made this habit, I realized a significant improvement in my creativity and conviction level to pursue my passions.

But why did I not rebuild this habit between 1990 and 2015, for full twenty-five years?

Because I knew, but I did not believe. And hence, I was not convinced of the power of morning habits. Once I realized, I launched a programme called '10x Success and Joys through the power of MMRG' under which I conduct a free session for anyone who wants to build this powerful habit. What gives me energy to conduct the sessions three days a week in early morning hours? It's the conviction coming out of my deep personal experience.

Second example: There are so many videos on the power of pursuing your passion. There are books, videos and podcasts shouting about the magical power of following your passion. But how many people can actually do this? Very few. This is again because they do not believe or have conviction in the power of passion. They either see others who also started pursuing their passion without actually knowing their passion and hence gave up midway, or they themselves do not have the courage to take tough actions and reveal the true powers hidden within them through the power of consistent actions. They see someone speaking in support of pursuing passion and then see others who say just the opposite. Both groups are right, as they are speaking based on their personal experiences. Success lies in the intensity of belief and conviction. Once you have these, you will find a way. If needed, you will learn new skills and new set of people to support you. If needed, you will take additional actions, but you will find a way. The path is full of challenges and success or failure depends on the person who wants to pursue passions.

One important aspect of self-improvement or self-transformation is – it depends more on the mentee or the student and less on the teacher, mentor or the coach. Jim Rohn had mentioned this in one of the talks – if he conducted a session for a group of people, only 10% would have been interested in buying his book and out of the people who bought the book, only 10% would have finished the book. Out of the people who finished the book, only 10% would have implemented at least a few lessons in their life. That brings us to a % hit rate of 0.001 or 0.1%. It is a mere coincidence that, broadly speaking, this also is the % of successful people in the world. This applies everywhere. If you choose a group of people at random and ask them to join you in building a great business, only 10% people would be interested in building a great business and out of these people, only 10% would have the discipline to take some actions every day for some time, at least till the time things are easy and downhill. Out of this group, only 10% would have the tenacity to keep taking actions even when things become uphill or challenging. These are the people who succeed in life. Again, you see – it's the same % of people who would be successful in creating a great new company. You can test this idea in any field. No surprises that only a small percentage of people actually succeed in creating a world which is fulfilling, enjoyable and inspiring. Others keep struggling all their life.

A wise man said – when the student is ready, teachers are everywhere. This is so true. When I came to the field of motivation and life transformation through coaching, writing and speaking, I thought I will transform the life of anyone and everyone. Soon, I realized, I could not have been farther from the truth. Let's start with an example of The Bhagvat Gita. Lord Krishna became the teacher only for Arjuna. Duryodhana, Karna, Dushashana and so many others were not ready to be the student and hence they could not see the coach in Krishna. The funny thing is – Lord Krishna or the coach is everywhere around you. But you can't see them unless you develop the hunger for learning and improving. Transformation depends on the student and not on the teacher. Recently, I was interacting with one of the old friends from my college days. He has been into IIT coaching and has taught many students to crack IIT and join some of the most reputed MNCs. He admitted openly – the success of any IIT coaching centre mostly (to the extent of 95%) depends on the student. 4% credit goes to the parent and only 1% credit goes to the teachers.

I also realized it very soon after getting into the field of coaching. I recall, in my initial days of conducting motivational sessions for the students of a reputed MBA college, I could easily see that some 10% students used to be connected to my teachings instantly. They used to ask questions and nod and smile whenever I made a point. Others used to just look around, as if given a chance, they could jump out of the windows and doors to go for a cup of coffee or tea in the nearby cafes. I also knew out of these 10% students, only 10% would actually take some actions at least till things would be easy and nice going. Later I realized that only 10% out of these students would actually be practising my teachings even after a year or so. That means, only 0.1% students would be taking actions despite facing challenges.

See, again you come to the same percentage

Now, let's extend this example. I experimented with this as I went to conduct a similar session for the students in the same MBA college. Three years had passed since I had conducted the previous session. It was new batch of students, but it was the similar group with same age group and preferences. This time, I was a new and improved version of myself, having written half a dozen books and having developed new realisations in life in the field of life transformation. Unlike last time, when I needed a whole bunch of slides to put my points forward, this time, I went without any presentation pack. Now, I had become a walking presentation as I had internalised so many concepts, real life examples and stories that I conducted a 12-hour workshop for various groups of students without using a single slide. I could connect with students a lot better this time. I smiled with them, engaged them in the process of learning and made them ask on the spot questions while answering to the questions giving on the spot examples. This time, I could see that almost 50% of them were engaged in the conversation. But again, out of these 50% of people, what percentage of students would have looked back at the learnings and done something about these after finishing the session? 10% of those 50%. Next, what % of people would have kept taking actions even after a year? Now you again come to a % of 10. So, in essence, we have 0.5% people - that is five times the earlier number of people – who took some actions. Hence, the teacher can increase the number of people who would see a transformation in their life, but what percentage of people we are talking about in general? It's a miniscule part indeed. Great news is – these small number of people also start impacting other lives and this is how the chain of goodness spreads. But majority percentage will still remain of those who don't want to change and this percentage is anywhere between 95% to 99%. This is the way it was hundreds and thousands of years ago (go back to the example of *The Bhagvat Gita*) and this is the way it's going be there for ever.

So, what is the morale of the story – the transformation depends more on the student and less on the teacher. The same is going to happen with this book as well. You know the % of people who would be transforming their life and doing something worthwhile after reading the book. Though the percentage looks pretty small, the great news is – with talks, marketing efforts and collaborations, we can see an ever-increasing number of the book thereby increasing the overall number of people who would be transforming their life in the society, the country and the world.

## Courage

Freedom from fear is your right, but are you ready to fight with all your might?

In movie *Neerja*, air hostess of the hijacked plane, after trying to regain her composure, takes a glass of drinking water and is about to move back to a nervous and thirsty passenger.

The hijacker comes in the way, looks at her menacingly and asks her not to carry water to anyone.

She says in a calm and stern voice, 'I will do my duty just like you are doing yours.'

This brings me to the single most critical factor for you to bring a positive transformation in your life.

And that is COURAGE!

Do you have the courage to do what is right and not what will make others happy?

Transformation is also about not being threatened by little setbacks in life which are anyway a part of the journey. The idea is to keep moving ahead with a renewed vigour and energy. The idea is to work and toil in late nights and early mornings when your scheming competitors are busy partying around thinking that they have won the 'battles'. The idea is to turn the tables on them when they least expected this to happen. While they try to upstage your plans, you are busy learning from setbacks and doubling the intensity of your thoughts and actions to be a success at what you do. The secret lies in doing what is right every day, day by day, without bothering about the outcomes of the journey. If the act is right, your goals will be soon in sight. Don't listen to people who talk about politicking and making others fail. Ultimately what wins is talent, hard work, passion and limitless energy to keep moving ahead. Ultimately the person who wins is the one who does not get distracted from his daily rituals. The person who wins is the one who always walks on the right path, without fearing the outcome. The person who wins is the one who will not get side-tracked by scheming people because he knows that the world is all about mediocre people who neither want to be great nor want to make others around them become greater. It's a crab mentality which is affecting the world around us. You need to stay focused towards your goals.

## The Price of Self-Transformation

You need to be ready to pay the price of transformation. It does not come without a price. Nothing in this world is free. Everything, every success story, every achievement and every moment of glory comes at a price which has to be paid. But the price is not even a fraction of the benefits which you are going to enjoy. I can say this from my personal experience. You should be willing to pay the price with a deep sense of gratitude, joyfulness and willingness. This is because the outcome is so vivacious, you will forget all the pains and sacrifices made on the way.

One price of transformation that you have to pay is to come out of the shadow of your mentor and come out in open sun. It's a process in which at the beginning, you need to seek navigation, motivation, support and constant push from your mentor or coach. Then you have to learn and implement the lessons taught to you. There will come a time when you have to move out of the shadow of your mentor. You have to be on your own. Just like your parents will take you in the journey of your life only till a certain distance. Beyond the point, you have to walk on the path alone. I lost my mother when I was twenty-five years. Then I lost my father when I turned thirty-six years. Till my parents were with me, I could not imagine a life without them. I was born in a small township and had grown under very careful upbringing of my parents. My father had given me all resources to study and be the best among all students. I never disappointed him. He never asked me to do anything other than my studies. This was because my father wanted me to use all my time for doing something I was very good at and that was studies. This also means how dependent I was on my parents. I grew up and after class 10, I was to get admission in another city which was far bigger than the town I had spent my entire childhood days in.

My father came to drop me in the city. We stayed in the home of one of my father's friends. I got admission in the best college in the city and it took a few days. Then I had to live in one of the hostels. I still recall, after I was put in the hostel with all my belongings organised, now it was the time for my father to leave me back. He had to go back to the same beautiful town I had spent the beautiful days of my childhood. I still remember, I had tears in my eyes when he came out to the main road before catching an autorickshaw. I was feeling scared at the mere thought of being left alone in this big bad city among completely unknown people. My father also was sad and I could see how desperately he was trying to hide his tearful eyes.

He was not sure how his son, who had been kept in such a well-protected environment where his only chores were studies, would survive with 'the life in a metro' where he had to arrange for his food, safety, security and shelter while doing his studies.

I still feel the fear and nervousness of living in a completely unknown city all on my own.

Years passed by and I lost both my parents one by one. I somehow, with each loss, gained courage and strength rather than losing a part of me. I built a better career in return of the price, which I had to pay. Today I know the price, which I had to pay – it was breaking my comfort zone. Today when I teach my mentees that nothing grows inside comfort zone, I understand why breaking my comfort zone was so necessary for me to grow into a more confident and self-dependent man. I am a family man and have my wife and children. We have houses in some of the most beautiful cities in India and I smile back at the thought of prices which I paid at each stage of my life and career. Later on, it became a habit for me to break my comfort zone. Every time I felt being too comfortable with the current status, I broke it. When I grew too comfortable in Tata Steel Limited, I broke my comfort zone and left the company to come to an entirely new company called Tata BlueScope Steel Limited, which had an entirely new culture. When I felt that I had grown too comfortable in Tata Group, I left the group to join an MNC. I left a small city of Jamshedpur to come to a larger city with many variables and uncertainties only to have a lifetime of experiences. My book is completely dedicated to this love for breaking comfort zones. Had I not kept changing my world, I would not have learnt so many lessons I am writing about in this book. My coach, my experiences, my publishers, my visits to crossword, my long-distance drives and just everything which has become a part of my life is due to my courageous decisions all through my life. I say this with a great degree of humility. I also know that this courage is still a tiny piece in comparison with the courage demonstrated by those who have transformed the world. You take any name and you will see a story of extreme courage in the face of life-threatening fear.

Courage is like daily sprinkle of water without which no tree of success can grow. Period.

Charles Darwin (1809–1882), by his own admission, was an average human being until he decided to undertake the most ambitious and difficult journey of his lifetime. In this journey, he was supposed to be away from his family and native town for more than five years. He was to spend all these years on a ship amidst some of the seasoned sailors who were to make fun of Charles Darwin for being too naïve, childish and 'impractical'. Before setting off on this journey, Charles Darwin had been rebuked by his father who said, 'You care for nothing, but shooting, dogs, and rat-catching, and you will be a disgrace to yourself and all your family.' Charles Darwin was good at no subject in the school. He was not interested in learning from books. But he loved learning from the outdoors. I am sure, had Darwin not broken his comfort zone by deciding to undertake the journey of the unknown in the ship HMS *Beagle*, he would not have become the person the world still talks of and will keep talking of. He is one of the best examples of how people are completely transformed by paying the price for it. When I decided to go through complete transformation, I was mentally ready for the price. For me, it was replacing my 'fun-filled' late evening TV time with early morning meditation, reading, writing and goal-reading time. And if you ask me, I do not consider this as the price at all. It is the most enjoyable moment of my life now. If I wake up late by an hour, I spend my entire day trying to retrieve that one hour.

For Mozart, the price came in the form of leaving his family and house and come to Paris where he lived on his own and learnt the art of piano. Had he stayed back at his home with family, his father would have made him play the same music again and again as that was the demand of the orchestra. Mozart loved creating new musical notes instead. He was first cajoled and then forced by his father, who used to work in an orchestra, to play the notes created by someone else to make a living in the orchestra. Mozart could not bear this and took the biggest risk of life to leave his family and home and rest is history. Mozart is a musical phenomenon of all times even after more than 200 years.

You look at the story of transformation of any great human being and you will find the same common thread in all such cases – everyone had paid the price before moving on and becoming a completely transformed person. Amitabh Bachchan's trademark deep baritone voice, tall, brooding persona and intense eyes, made him an ideal 'Angry Young Man', setting him apart from the cluster of Bollywood's lover boys. However, his unconventional looks did work against him at the beginning of his Bollywood career, but he stayed around long enough to be become the icon of the Indian film industry. He paid the price by spending nights on benches in Mumbai and getting rejected by many directors for his unconventional looks and voice. But once he got the first break, he never looked back. He was a completely transformed person who made a unique record of six blockbuster movies in the same year 1978. So total was his dominance on the Indian movie scene in the 1970s and 1980s that the French director François Truffaut called him a 'one-man industry'.

This is called true transformation – from sleeping on a bench to becoming one-man industry and remaining so for years altogether.

With all that we have covered in the book, you have all the resources for leading an improved, transformed and inspired life.

The most important journey of transformation will start now as you finish reading the book.

The difference will lie in the way you will behave now.

Will you be an action taker or the one who is too lazy to act on just so many lessons we have written about in all 14 chapters in this book.

You will never need any other book for permanent transformation of your life even if you act on 25% of the lessons in this book.

Yes. It's true!!!

Wishing you great success, joys and health in all your endeavours.